ONE NATION 'ABOVE' GOD

Book #5 in the *What Works* Book Series

"And there arose another generation
after them who did not know the LORD."

JUDGES 2:10

ONE NATION 'ABOVE' GOD

SHANE ALAN IDLEMAN

One Nation 'Above' God

E.P.
**El Paseo
Publications**

Published by El Paseo Publications
www.elpaseopublications.com

Cover design by Eric Walljasper
Interior design by Sandi Welch

The quote on the cover, *And there arose another generation after them who did not know the LORD,* is a paraphrase of Judges 2:10.

All biblical references are from the New King James version of the Bible, published by Thomas Nelson, 1995. Scriptures and quotes within quotation marks are exact quotes; whereas, paraphrased Scriptures and quotes are italicized.

We make every effort to attribute the source of a quote to the correct author. If there is no acknowledgment, the author either wrote the quote or we could not determine the source. Not all quotes are referenced in the endnotes if the exact source could not be verified, or if the text identifies the source.

ISBN-13: 978-0-9713393-5-4
ISBN-10: 0-9713393-5-X

Library of Congress Control Number: 2007909896
Printed in the United States of America

DEDICATION

Passing the Baton

This book is dedicated to my mother, Diane Idleman.
Thank you for the many days, nights, weeks, months,
and years invested in me and in our family;
may it return a hundredfold. Aside from the Lord,
in the words of Abraham Lincoln: *All that I am,
and all that I'll ever be, I owe to my mother.*

This book is also dedicated to my wife and children;
the joy of being a husband and father is incredible.
My prayer is that our children will take God's Word into
all areas of their lives and allow the spiritual baton to pass
from one generation to the next.

"But we have forgotten God, and we have vainly imagined, in the deceitfulness of our hearts, that all these blessings were produced by some superior wisdom and virtue of our own."[1]

—ABRAHAM LINCOLN (1809-1865)
Proclamation of a National Day of Prayer, 1863

ENDORSEMENTS

"America's founders created 'one nation under God.' But modern elitists are trying to create 'one nation above God' (if that were possible). Shane Idleman, in his book, *One Nation 'Above' God,* spells out what's at stake if we continue down this totally wrong path."

—D. JAMES KENNEDY
Coral Ridge Ministries, Fort Lauderdale, Florida.

"What America is and has been was the result of previous generations; everything she will become depends on the rising generation. Shane fully understands this and has provided our next generation of leaders with an understanding of the principles that will keep America great. This book can help secure America's future as 'one nation under God.' "

—DAVID BARTON
President and Founder, WallBuilders, Aledo, Texas.

"One Nation 'Above' God is a must read for all ages!"

—TONY PERKINS
President, Family Research Council, Washington, D.C.

"Shane Idleman's book, *One Nation 'Above' God,* serves as a wake-up call to Christian Americans that sitting on the sidelines is no longer an option for those who love their country and love their God. The blessings of freedom we have enjoyed in America are a direct result of the foundation of Judeo-Christian principles laid down by our forefathers. As our culture slowly chips away at these foundations, our nation is at risk of collapsing from within. But there is hope! And Shane Idleman's book points all Christians in the right direction toward achieving change."

—PETER LILLBACK
President, The Providence Forum, and Senior Pastor,
Proclamation Presbyterian Church, Pennsylvania.

"One Nation 'Above' God makes a compelling case that almost all of America's current troubles are rooted in the growing abandonment of Judeo-Christian values. Shane Idleman's heartfelt call to young and old to live an upright life for God is refreshingly genuine and unpretentious—and therefore powerful."

—DAVID KUPELIAN
Author of "The Marketing of Evil," and
Managing Editor of WorldNetDaily.com.

TABLE OF CONTENTS

AN IMPORTANT NOTE
FROM THE PUBLISHER

EL PASEO PUBLICATIONS IS COMMITTED to quality in publication—to inspire, educate, and encourage the highest standard of excellence through written communication.

One Nation 'Above' God is the fifth book in the *What Works* book series. (Additional books in the series are listed in the *About the Author* section.) We hope you find this concise resource both thought provoking and challenging.

El Paseo Publications has diligently attempted to accurately represent all references. America's founding leaders have been largely misrepresented in recent years, but after an exhaustive research effort, in our opinion, the intent of countless early Americans and many of the Founders was to honor God and to preserve His Word. Granted, there is a danger in labeling all the Founders Christians, and in calling all the founding documents "Christian" documents. Doing so can lead to national idolatry and arrogance. As the author states, "To adequately evaluate America's heritage, we must turn back time a few hundred years before 1776 when the seeds of America's political system were being planted."

We recognize there are varying opinions in the Christian community regarding the religious beliefs of some of the

Founding Fathers. One of our goals, therefore, is not to elevate the Founders or America's heritage, but to point solely to God's Word as the solid foundation on which our lives rest.

Not all those quoted in this book are Founding Fathers. For the purpose of this book, a Founder was someone who profoundly impacted or influenced the establishment, organization, and founding of America.

We've taken many avenues to make this resource as comprehensive and complete as possible without adding copious information. Although we've attempted to be as accurate as possible, as with any other book, there may be mistakes typographically or in subject matter; if you identify any, we encourage you to contact us. Not all quotes are referenced in the endnotes if the exact source could not be verified, or if the text identifies the source. Brackets [ ] were used when the author added clarification, or when capitalization or verb tense changes were made.

We have also modernized certain words to aid readability. For example, in the 1642 *Rules and Precepts of Harvard,* maine, eternall, and bottome, were changed to main, eternal, and bottom. Additionally, some ellipses have been removed to aid readability. In such instances, the intended meaning of the quotation was not altered or changed, and the full quote was noted in the *Endnotes* section. We encourage those who might use these quotes in the future to be aware of these changes and note them.

The majority of the content found in this book was

taken directly from *What Works for Young Adults* © 2007; however, some of the material has been reorganized and updated, and numerous additions have been made.

El Paseo Publications, and the author, do not necessarily agree with, or endorse, every opinion and/or belief expressed in the *Recommended Resources* section. We do, however, encourage readers to educate and equip themselves regarding the issues.

Scriptures and quotes within quotation marks are exact quotes; whereas, paraphrased Scriptures and quotes are often italicized. In some cases, only portions of Scriptures and quotes are referenced. **Both the author and the publisher acknowledge the distinction between God's instructions to the nation of Israel in the Old Testament, and His plan for the church today. Therefore, all Scriptures should be read in their complete context whenever possible.**

HOW TO USE THIS BOOK

CONTEMPORARY STUDENTS OFTEN MISS THE critical connection between America's unparalleled greatness, her rise to world leadership, and the spiritual foundation that made it possible. This should concern us: *The ideas of the classroom in one generation will create the ideas of government within the next.* For this reason, this book can also be used as an educational resource for teachers, homeschoolers, churches, family devotions, and Bible study groups.

The short chapters are designed to help readers obtain correct information about the faith and values that gave birth to the freest nation on earth. Had we better known the spiritual history of America, as well as the writings of early Americans, it would have been difficult to accept many of the false claims leveled against the Founders and other early Americans.

The *Wisdom Worth Repeating* section, near the back of the book, lists several thought provoking quotes that do not appear in the main body of the book.

—Located at the end of each chapter—

• *Group Study Questions* highlight important points from each chapter. Our hope is that each question will encourage dialogue and motivate the reader to search the Bible and historical documents for the answers.

• *Recommended Resources* are additional resources for those interested in learning more about a particular topic. From George Washington and freemasonry, to Christian ethics and political involvement—from separation of church and state to the motivation behind the Declaration of Independence, this section lists several noteworthy resources.

• *Reflection & Journaling* allows you to elaborate on the group study questions and/or journal your thoughts and prayers. Date your entry; include what you learned, and how certain aspects of the chapter can be directly applied to your life.

ACKNOWLEDGMENTS

MY DEEPEST GRATITUDE TO my wife, Morgan, my daughter, Aubrey, and my son, Shane; all have been a tremendous blessing. I thank God for a wonderful family; they are the true treasures in life.

In addition to my mother, who was acknowledged earlier (the *What Works* book series would not be what it is today had it not been for her insight), I also want to acknowledge my father, Jim Idleman, who died of a heart attack at age 54. He inspired me more than he could have known. I'll be forever grateful for the experiences we shared, the lessons I learned, and the man I became as a result of the time we spent together.

A special thanks to my brother, Ryan, and his wife, Christina, along with Christian and Austin, as well as my sister, Meredith, her husband, Francisco Jabier, her son, Hayden, and daughter, Felicity. I also want to thank Morgan's family for their support and acceptance: Augie, Linda, Alexis, and Curt, as well as Leah, Shawn, Jessica, Allison, and Kelsey.

Additional thanks to those who offered endorsements, and to the late D. James Kennedy for his inspiration and encouragement.

Appreciation is also offered to those who provided support, comments, and suggestions, including Alex Montoya, Ralf Augstroze, Aleda Swartzendruber, Ricardo and Yolanda Romero, Ed Smith, Brian Ingalls, Mike McCormick, Randy McMillen, Sean Appleton, Keith Deaville, Mike Morris, Josh Hueser, Grant Poole, and Rich Cowe. Thank you for taking the time to thoroughly review the manuscript and/or offer feedback and encouragement; it was greatly appreciated.

Although unaware of their influence, several Christian leaders contributed to my spiritual development through-out the years, and more specifically, to this book. A special thanks to David Barton, Alistair Begg, James Dobson, Billy and Franklin Graham, David Jeremiah, John MacArthur, James MacDonald, Roy Moore, J.I. Packer, John Piper, Paul E. Sheppard, Chuck Smith, and Ravi Zacharias, to name only a few.

Legacies That Live On

The following men are no longer with us; however, their legacies continue to live. They have not only been an incredible inspiration to me, but to countless others as well. A special note of appreciation for the following:

• *Jonathan Edwards* (1703-1758), minister and theologian who contributed greatly to the Great Awakening—a spiritual movement in America in the 1730s and 1740s that breathed new spiritual life into the Colonies.

• *John Wesley* (1703-1791), recognized Founder of the Methodists, and a key figure in the Great Awakening.

• *George Whitefield* (1714-1770), primary evangelist during the Great Awakening.

• *Charles Haddon Spurgeon* (1834-1892), considered one of the best preachers of the nineteenth century.

• *D.L. Moody* (1837-1899), considered one of the greatest evangelists of the nineteenth century.

• *A.W. Tozer* (1897-1963), a bold Christian Missionary Alliance minister who authored several inspiring books.

• *Martin Luther King, Jr.* (1929-1968), Christian leader, and one of the founders of America's Civil Rights Movement.

• *D. Martyn Lloyd-Jones* (1899-1981), a theologian, as well as a powerful Welsh preacher.

• *Adrian Rogers* (1931-2005), Pastor of Belleview Baptist Church in Memphis, Tennessee, for 33 years. His character and ministry inspired Christians worldwide.

"Remember ever, and always, that your country was founded by the stern old Puritans whose first act on touching the soil of the new world was to offer on bended knees thanksgiving to Almighty God."[2]

—HENRY WILSON (1812-1875)
18TH U.S. Vice President

INTRODUCTION

As I complete this book, war rages in the Middle East, and the potential for nuclear war intensifies. America is divided on many fronts. Where are the answers? How will the future and security of America unfold in the days to come?

My previous books address personal issues. This book, however, recognizes the biblical foundation that once guided America. These principles are the foundation on which America's success rests. My objective is not to be judgmental or negative, but to expose the danger of striving to be *One Nation 'Above' God*. My intention is not to endorse a political party, policy, or candidate, or to elevate America's Founders, but to point to the power of Scripture to shape an individual, as well as a nation. Who we are in our personal lives will reflect who we are as a nation.

In July 1776, during what many have called "one of the greatest historical events of all time," the Continental Congress of the United States of America officially declared independence, and its reputation as a great country was born. Despite the beliefs of some, early Americans were not all renegades and rebels. For decades the Colonists tried to cooperate with the King, but, as time passed, it became evident that change was necessary. Great Britain needed to relinquish her oppressive control. **Although controversy surrounds the biblical justification for the American Revolution, the Founders did not initiate the conflict, and thus, believed that they had biblical justification for their actions.** *The Founders viewed the Revolution as a defensive conflict rather than an offensive war.* After peaceful and legal redress had been exhausted, they moved toward independence from the King and dependence on God.

> My intention is not to endorse a political party, policy, or candidate, or to elevate America's Founders, but to point to the power of Scripture to shape an individual, as well as a nation. Who we are in our personal lives will reflect who we are as a nation.

Although the history of America is marked with disappointments, tragedies, mistakes, and failures, my intent is not to write about the history of America, but to unapologetically proclaim the truth behind her success.

As the moral and cultural war rages between our shores, the need to be awakened from our spiritual slumber has never been greater. **"Where the battle rages, there the loyalty of the soldier is tested" (Martin Luther)**. This battle is for the very soul of our nation. It's our choice—stand or fall.

—*Shane Alan Idleman*

"There is no nation on earth powerful enough to accomplish our overthrow. Our destruction, should it come at all, will be from another quarter. From the inattention of the people to the concerns of their government, from their carelessness and negligence."[3]

—DANIEL WEBSTER (1782-1852)
U.S. Secretary of State, 1841-42; 1850-52

ONE

The Deterioration of a Nation

Mandatory Euthanasia Bill

WASHINGTON, D.C.—WHAT MANY CALL GENOCIDE, Congress calls necessary to curtail rising healthcare costs. In the hope of reclaiming financial stability, many legislators plan to sign a mandatory Euthanasia Bill. In defense of the Bill, some State Representatives claim that abortion has helped to offset rising health care costs. This new legislation will include those with terminal or chronic illnesses—life will be terminated when rehabilitation is uncertain, and/or when lingering illnesses threaten the economy. Those with criminal records, and the elderly, are also being considered. The bill is expected to take effect late next year.

Congress Lowers Age of Sexual Consent

WASHINGTON, D.C.—Congress will vote later this year to lower the age of sexual consent to 12. Members have agreed to consider new research indicating that sex between children and adults may be beneficial. Although this new research appears problematic and has been described as biased, it may have prompted a trend in the lower courts to assign convicted pedophiles lesser penalties such as community service, or rehabilitation, for committing lewd acts with children. This movement may explain why many judges now offer rehabilitation rather than imprisonment. Even though research confirms that punishment reduces crime, many appear eager to facilitate this new trend.

Same-sex Marriage Exceeds Traditional Marriage

WASHINGTON, D.C.—Same-sex marriage now exceeds traditional marriage in some states. As a result, words such as "mom" and "dad" are being changed to "partner 1" and "partner 2." Congress, however, is concerned that decreased birth rates will affect the nation's economy. In response, partners will be required to explore creative procreation options. Additionally, traditional families will be limited to two children. If couples fail to comply, infanticide may be considered.

Zero Tolerance for Christians

WASHINGTON, D.C.—Homeland Security reports that Christianity is now under control. A recent poll indicates that fewer than two percent of the population report adhering to Christian beliefs and biblical absolutes. This decrease is attributed to a successful "Zero Tolerance" policy, which includes hate-speech legislation, outlawing use of the Bible, incarceration for Christians, heavy taxation on evangelical churches, and media scrutiny of anyone associated with the Christian faith. Additionally, many biblical terms dealing with marriage, sexual orientation, and family values are now identified as hate speech and cannot be used in public.

Although fictitious, these imaginary headlines may be more fact than fiction if America continues to ignore the warning signs.

At the time of this writing, it is said that we live in the greatest country in the world, but the success we cherish is not the result of chance. Many early Americans, including most of the Founders, understood that in order for a nation to thrive and prosper, God's Word must provide the basis for the government and the welfare of society. I'm not suggesting a theocracy, nor were the Founders, but I am suggesting a return to Judeo-Christian values. Just as water rapidly eroded the banks of the mighty Colorado River and created a vast Grand Canyon, America's current belief system (relativism) has eroded her foundation and created a moral void.

WHILE WE ARE CONCERNED WITH TERRORIST ATTACKS, AND RIGHTLY SO, THERE IS A GREATER THREAT FROM CORRUPTION WITHIN. WE, LIKE THE MIGHTY ROMAN EMPIRE THAT COLLAPSED CENTURIES AGO, ARE CRUMBLING FROM WITHIN.

Interestingly enough, the stability of America is one of the top concerns on the minds of many today. There was a time in recent history when America felt secure knowing that the most formidable enemies were abroad. Not so today. While we are concerned with terrorist attacks, and rightly so, there is a greater threat from corruption within. We, like the mighty Roman Empire that collapsed centuries ago, are crumbling from within. There are people and groups who are strongly committed to the destruction of anything rooted in our nation's Christian heritage. They attempt to be "one nation 'above' God," rather than "one nation 'under' God." Scripture identifies this as foolishness, self-exaltation, and arrogance—the downfall of nations.

There is a saying that *one generation plants trees for the next generation*. I'm concerned that instead of planting, we are removing and destroying the very covering that protects us. As a result, our legacy as a great and noble nation has all but been forgotten. For instance, most schools no longer teach students about the spiritual foundation that has guided America throughout her history. Consequently, America's moral and religious heritage is often deleted, grossly distorted, or revised altogether. As stated earlier: Students often miss the critical connection between America's unparalleled greatness, her rise to world leadership, and the spiritual foundation that made it possible. This should concern us. *The ideas of the classroom in one generation will create the ideas of government within the next.*

> LET IT NOT BE SAID OF US TODAY: AND THERE AROSE ANOTHER GENERATION AFTER THEM WHO DID NOT KNOW THE LORD (JUDGES 2:10).

Today, our culture promotes relativism, and man does what is right in his own eyes. Again, according to Scripture, to his own destruction. **God's Word says to confront, confess, and turn from our sins; relativism encourages us to ignore, overlook, and continue in them.**

Although this position may seem radical or extreme, we are living in extremely critical times. Make no mistake about it: We are witnessing the rapid deterioration of a nation right before our eyes. But there is hope: 2 Chronicles 7:14 calls out from the past with resounding clarity to America today: *If My people will humble themselves and pray and seek My face and turn from their wicked ways, I will hear from heaven, forgive their sins, and heal their land.*

There are times to encourage, motivate, and uplift, but there are also times to confront, challenge, and contend for what is right—that time is now. Let it not be said of us today: *And there arose another generation after them who did not know the LORD* (Judges 2:10).

GROUP
STUDY QUESTIONS

1. If America continues to ignore the warning signs, is it possible that the imaginary headlines could become a reality?

2. How many of those headlines, do you believe, are currently being discussed, and to what degree?

3. Do you agree that the success we cherish in America is not the result of chance? Explain.

4. Do you believe that in order for a nation to thrive and prosper, God's Word must provide the basis for the government and the welfare of society? Elaborate.

5. Why are some biblical terms dealing with marriage and sexual orientation considered hate speech? What is often the motive behind such legislation?

6. How has America's current belief system (relativism) eroded her biblical foundation?

7. Although there is a distinction between God's plan for the nation of Israel in the Old Testament, and His plan for the church today, how does 2 Chronicles 7:14 offer hope for our time? What responsibilities do we have?

RESPONSE

1. _____
_____
_____

2. _____
_____
_____

3. _____
_____
_____

4. _____
_____
_____

5. _____
_____
_____

6. _____
_____
_____

7. _____
_____
_____

"Blessed is the nation whose God is the LORD"
(Psalm 33:12).

RECOMMENDED RESOURCES

The Marketing of Evil, by David Kupelian, is an exceptional resource that outlines how radicals, elitists, and pseudo-experts sell us corruption disguised as freedom, and what this means to the future of America.

Of Plymouth Plantation, by William Bradford, is an eyewitness account that accurately traces the history of the New Plymouth Settlement in the early hours of American history. It demonstrates why God's Word must provide the basis for the government and the welfare of society.

Pray for Our Nation, published by Harrison House, is a small booklet containing scriptural prayers focused on revival.

America—To Pray or Not to Pray, by David Barton, reveals what happens to a society when biblical principles are separated from public affairs.

REFLECTION & JOURNALING

Date _____

Additional Thoughts & Chapter Highlights

_____

_____

_____

_____

_____

_____

_____

_____

_____

_____

_____

Prayers & Practical Application

_____

_____

_____

_____

_____

_____

_____

_____

_____

_____

_____

_____

"And if a sparrow cannot fall to the ground without His notice, is it probable that an empire can rise without His aid?"[4]

—BENJAMIN FRANKLIN (1706-1790)
Founding Father, Political Theorist, Inventor

TWO

Keep the Roots Alive

As a child, I was captivated by the stories that my grandfather told about life on the farm in Oklahoma in the early 1900s. The images that I've held are not those of pleasant surroundings or ideal conditions; they are impressions of twelve-hour days spent working the land, dust storms that could devastate a crop, blistered and sunburned skin, and poverty unlike most Americans know today. Life, in general, was harder then, but interestingly enough, families seemed stronger—it was a time when the roots of commitment, integrity, and honesty ran deep. A handshake and a man's word were generally good enough.

I'm not suggesting that we return to that time in history, but that we learn from the past and strongly encourage those same character traits today. *A nation, like a tree, is easily destroyed when the roots are removed.*

Today, careers are built at the cost of the family. Being a family man or a stay-at-home mom is often frowned upon.

Ironically, **the strength of the nation will depend on the stability of the family.** Noted author and speaker, Josh McDowell, once stated that the reason so many young people are losing ground in the area of spiritual truth is because their parents are not involved in teaching them in word or action. He added, "One of the most common questions I get is, 'How could we live for Christ, when we don't want the Christ that our parents have?'"[5] Wow, that should force us all to ask, "Who am I influencing, and who's influencing me?" When the destruction of the family is coming from within the same walls that were designed to protect it, it's time for change.

> WHEN THE DESTRUCTION OF THE FAMILY IS COMING FROM WITHIN THE SAME WALLS THAT WERE DESIGNED TO PROTECT IT, IT'S TIME FOR CHANGE.

On that note, let's briefly discuss homosexuality—some legislators have attempted to redefine marriage and the family in order to accommodate this lifestyle. I believe Christians err when they embrace one of two extremes. At one extreme are those who insult, or who are violent toward those trapped in this lifestyle; homosexuality appears at the top of their sin list; there is very little love or compassion. The other extreme excuses this sin and looks the other way.

Biblically speaking, homosexuality, like all sexual sin, is morally wrong and harmful. In Matthew 15:19, when Jesus said, *Out of the heart comes evil thoughts, adulteries, fornications . . . these defile a man,* He condemned all sexual activity outside of marriage. The word for "fornication" in the Greek is *porneia*—this is where the word "pornography" comes from; it includes all illicit sex. Many other passages in the Bible contain strong warnings against any sexual activity outside of marriage as well. Sadly, it's impossible to un-know what is known. Think about that: Sexual experiences cannot be un-done. Each time we engage in illicit sex, we add emotional weight to our lives. Sex is good and God-ordained, but only within the context of marriage between a man and a woman. That's how God designed it. God's principles are guardrails through the canyons of life. They don't prevent us from enjoying life; they protect us from falling.

You may say, "Times change." And you are correct, but God's standards do not. The sin that once amazed us now amuses us; just look at what is considered "entertainment" today. When sin begins to amuse us, we are dangerously close to the edge—"Woe to those who call evil good, and good evil" (Isaiah 5:20). No matter how many laws are

GOD'S PRINCIPLES ARE GUARDRAILS THROUGH THE CANYONS OF LIFE. THEY DON'T PREVENT US FROM ENJOYING LIFE; THEY PROTECT US FROM FALLING.

passed in favor of same-sex marriage, it will not change God's mind. *I am the Lord thy God—I change not* (Malachi 3:6); yet, the goal of some is to justify homosexuality, adultery, and pre-marital sex. It's been said that if you tell a lie long enough, and often enough, people will begin to believe it. And isn't that true.

Granted, we should have compassion, but at the same time, we should not condone or excuse this type of sin any more than we condone or excuse any other sin such as adultery or fornication.

In reality, one of the greatest misunderstandings is in the concept of "individual rights." For example, pornography and other forms of so called "personal expression" that harm individuals as well as society, do not fit within the concept of exercising personal rights—logically, biblically, or historically. As a matter of fact, many cases of sexual violence can be traced directly back to pornography. *Personal rights were intended to operate freely, but only within the framework of social responsibility.* **We will always have the "freedom" to choose, but no one has the "right" to do what is wrong—no one!**

> SEXUAL SIN UNDERMINES HEALTH, AND OFTEN RESULTS IN THE DEATH OF A FAMILY, A MARRIAGE, AND THE INTEGRITY OF AN INDIVIDUAL—THE ENTIRE FAMILY LOSES. THAT'S WHAT SIN DOES; IT DRAWS THE LIFE OUT OF YOU, AND THOSE CLOSEST TO YOU.

Abortion and illicit sex are now determined by personal preference rather than by God's Word and social responsibility. Pornography is commonly protected as an expression of free speech while school prayer is often banned. Our society clearly reflects man's digression from God. This detour cannot produce safe, secure living. **The spiritual state of a nation simply reflects the spiritual state of her people—** spiritual decay undermines stability. When the family deteriorates, the deterioration of the nation is close at hand. Sexual sin undermines health, and often results in the death of a family, a marriage, and the integrity of an individual—the entire family loses. That's what sin does; it draws the life out of you, and those closest to you.

It's been said that culture is religion externalized. In other words, the culture around us simply reflects who and what we value. As things stand, the future of America will be an atmosphere of even greater intolerance toward those committed to God's ways, absolute truth, and traditional values. Ironically, groups that promote "tolerance" often lack tolerance for those who hold opposing views.

> WOODROW WILSON RIGHTLY SAID, "A NATION WHICH DOES NOT REMEMBER WHAT IT WAS YESTERDAY, DOES NOT KNOW WHAT IT IS TODAY, NOR WHAT IT IS TRYING TO DO."

If we fail to return to our biblical roots, we will lose a rich harvest of God's blessings and experience the pain of regret. But in order to take the initial steps to regain lost ground, it's important to understand why America was established, and it's equally important to note just how far we have drifted from the original intent of the founding principles. Woodrow Wilson rightly said, "A nation which does not remember what it was yesterday, does not know what it is today, nor what it is trying to do."[6]

I'm a firm believer that if we don't water the roots, the plants will die. As a kid during the summer, one of my jobs was to water the flowers that lined our front and back patios.

It was a simple job, but I was easily bored and anxious to finish. After quickly sprinkling the plants now and then for a few weeks, most of the flowers withered and died.

> SOME MAY BE OFFENDED BY AMERICA'S CHRISTIAN HERITAGE, BUT THAT DOES NOT GIVE THEM THE RIGHT TO REMOVE GOD FROM AMERICA'S HISTORY.

Rather than a lecture, my mother felt the best way to teach me responsibility and the need to soak the roots was to have me replace the flowers with my allowance. I learned a valuable lesson that summer: *Keep the roots alive.* In the same way, if we fail to keep America's spiritual roots alive, the fruit of that blessing will wither and die. Let us not forget: **America did not produce the blessings of liberty and freedom—liberty and freedom produced the blessings of America.**

Nearly 400 years ago, many sacrificed their lives and their families to promote religious freedom, and America was born. Many of those early Americans understood God's design for a prosperous life—they were not found in government, but in God alone—it was on this foundation that America was built. Some may be offended by America's Christian heritage, but that does not give them the right to remove God from America's history.

Fortunately, God will continue to call from each generation those who will support His principles. I believe that many today are called to support these truths. John Chalfant, a member of the Council for National Policy, said the following in his book *America—A Call to Greatness:* "If we participate in dragging down our country by refusing to become involved when we are commanded to be virtuous and to let our convictions be known, do we deserve to be free?" The price of freedom is never free. The moral state of our nation cannot be left to chance. We must keep the roots alive.

GROUP
STUDY QUESTIONS

1. Does the strength of the nation depend on the stability of the family? Explain your position.

2. Comment on this statement: "Times change, but God's standards do not." List examples of enduring biblical truths.

3. Do you agree that when sin begins to amuse us we are dangerously close to the edge? Why, why not?

4. If culture is religion externalized, what does our culture reveal about America today? What do we value and cherish?

5. What was Woodrow Wilson trying to convey: "A nation which does not remember what it was yesterday, does not know what it is today, nor what it is trying to do"?

6. Were you aware that personal "rights" were originally intended to operate freely, but only within the framework of social responsibility?

7. How can we exercise our rights and still be socially responsible? What is the difference between the "freedom" to choose and the "right" to choose?

RESPONSE

1. _____
_____
_____

2. _____
_____
_____

3. _____
_____
_____

4. _____
_____
_____

5. _____
_____
_____

6. _____
_____
_____

7. _____
_____
_____

"Blessed is the nation whose God is the LORD"
(Psalm 33:12).

RECOMMENDED RESOURCES

Marriage Under Fire, by Dr. James Dobson, describes why the definition of marriage should not be broadened or modernized. This book provides a well-defined guide for the preservation of traditional values in America today.

The Light and the Glory, by Peter Marshall and David Manuel, reviews the providential history of America, and shows why early Americans followed God's design for a prosperous life.

America's Providential History, by Mark A. Beliles and Stephen K. McDowell, outlines the providential view of history that was held by most early Americans.

America—A Call to Greatness, by John W. Chalfant, passionately captures the essence of Christianity as it relates to love of country and devotion to God's Word.

REFLECTION & JOURNALING

Date _____

Additional Thoughts & Chapter Highlights

_____
_____
_____
_____
_____
_____
_____
_____
_____
_____
_____
_____

Prayers & Practical Application

_____
_____
_____
_____
_____
_____
_____
_____
_____
_____
_____
_____
_____

"From the discovery of this continent to the present hour, there is a single voice making this affirmation . . . that this is a Christian nation."[7]

—THE U.S. SUPREME COURT, 1892

THREE

Is America a Christian Nation?

Let's begin by answering this question. As we do, it's important not to begin with the *Declaration of Independence* era (1776) as some do. For example, many point out, and rightly so, that some of the Framers of the Constitution were "religious" but not Christians. They use this argument to suggest that America was not founded on Christian principles, and that many of the founding documents in the late 1700s supported a broad range of views and beliefs rather than Christian doctrine. However, America's roots were established much earlier.

To adequately evaluate America's heritage, we must turn back time hundreds of years before 1776 when the seeds of our political system were being planted. The Pilgrims and Puritans, deeply committed to the Judeo-Christian faith and strongly influenced by Christian principles, emerged when the religious climate in Europe changed in the early 1500s. This was a time when many Christians returned to the authority of God's Word and the purity of biblical doctrine. These two groups eventually arrived in America in the early 1600s. Their prayers, journals, and writings, such as the *Mayflower Compact*, indicate that their intent was the furtherance of the *good news* (Gospel) of Christ and His teachings. Therefore, we must draw the conclusion that America was influenced greatly by the Judeo-Christian faith and the Bible.

With that said, I'm hesitant to label America a "Christian nation." Christians are followers of Christ, whereas a nation is a group of people who share a common identity, and often, a common origin. Some of the founders, such as Thomas Jefferson and Benjamin Franklin, were not considered Christians. *For this reason, America was not a Christian nation in the sense that every citizen or Founder was a Christian or was required to be one, but America is often labeled a Christian nation because her foundation was built on biblical principles and Christian character.*

Newsweek magazine, on December 27, 1982, in an article entitled, *How the Bible Made America*, made this revealing statement, "Historians are discovering that the Bible, perhaps even more than the Constitution, is our founding document." Undoubtedly, the Bible is the solid rock upon which our republic rests. For those who doubt this and believe that statements in the *Declaration of Independence* such as "the laws of nature and of nature's God" were products of the enlightenment, deism, or secularism, you may want to read quotes from founders such as Alexander Hamilton, Noah Webster, John Jay, William Findley, Rufus King, and James Wilson. All attested to the fact that "the laws of nature and of nature's God" refer to laws given by God Himself. *John Quincy Adams stated that the phrase assumes the existence of a God, the moral ruler of the universe, and a rule of right and wrong.* As a matter of fact, if a proposed article for the Constitution was not supported by, or rooted in the Bible, it was not considered. **In their early writings, many of the Founding Fathers quoted or referenced the Bible nearly four times more than any other source.**[8]

No enlightenment, deism, or secularism here—only God and His Word.

To understand the core values of a nation, one must simply look to the beliefs set forth during its conception, and, in the case of America, during the transitional years of the American Revolution. Judge for yourself how far we have drifted from the original intent of early Americans. Consider the following:

> "Historians are discovering that the Bible, perhaps even more than the Constitution, is our founding document."
>
> *Newsweek* magazine
> December 27, 1982

Then: First introduced in 1766, William Blackstone's *Commentaries on the Laws*, served as the legal reference for the Founders, as well as for many early American lawyers. Blackstone's commentaries were deeply rooted in biblical principles. It's been said that Blackstone was the first to use the phrase, "the laws of nature and of nature's God."

Now: "It is unconstitutional for students to see the Ten Commandments since they might read, meditate upon, respect, or obey them."[9]

Then: John Jay, the first Chief Justice of the U.S. Supreme Court, said, "Unto Him who is the author and giver of all good, I render sincere and humble thanks for His manifold and unmerited blessings, and especially for our redemption and salvation by His beloved Son."[10]

Now: In 1995, a District judge in Texas decreed that any student saying the name of Jesus during school graduation ceremonies would be jailed.[11]

> JOHN JAY, THE FIRST CHIEF JUSTICE OF THE U.S. SUPREME COURT, SAID, "UNTO HIM WHO IS THE AUTHOR AND GIVER OF ALL GOOD, I RENDER SINCERE AND HUMBLE THANKS FOR HIS MANIFOLD AND UNMERITED BLESSINGS, AND ESPECIALLY FOR OUR REDEMPTION AND SALVATION BY HIS BELOVED SON."

Then: Noah Webster, the Founding Father of American Scholarship and Education, said, "In my view, the Christian religion is the most important and one of the first things in which all children, under a free government, ought to be instructed . . . ."[12] He believed so strongly in this that he often gave Scripture references when he defined words in his colossal work: *American Dictionary of the English Language.* (I highly recommend the 1828 edition of this helpful resource.)

Now: Many students are criticized when they read their Bibles in public, or at school. Christianity is challenged, mocked, and ridiculed while most other beliefs are accepted and embraced. Sadly, in order to be politically correct, Noah

Webster's Scripture references have been withdrawn from recent editions.

Then: The *Delaware Constitution* initially required that everyone appointed to public office must say, "I do profess faith in God the Father, and in the Lord Jesus Christ his only Son . . . ." Many other Constitutions such as Maryland, New Jersey, Virginia, and Connecticut all acknowledged their reliance on God.[13]

Now: Those who run for office and profess a faith in Jesus Christ are viewed as fanatical and/or extreme, and are often criticized by the media.

Then: Early Americans felt that it was impossible to rightly govern the world without God and the Bible. They often petitioned God for guidance, direction, and encouragement. Fisher Ames, author of the *First Amendment*, openly declared, "Should not the Bible regain the place it once held as a school book?"[14]

Now: Bible displays, as well as Ten Commandment monuments, are often ruled unconstitutional in courthouses and other public places. Mr. Ames would no doubt disagree with these rulings.

Then: In 1790, Dr. Benjamin Rush, signer of the *Declaration of Independence*, said this about public schools, "But the religion I mean to recommend in this place is that of the New Testament . . . ."[15]

Now: Most public schools avoid doctrines of the New Testament. In *Roberts v. Madigan* (1989), for example, the court ruled: "It is unconstitutional for a classroom library to contain books which deal with Christianity, or for a teacher to be seen with a personal copy of the Bible at school."[16] (Granted, courts have ruled that the Bible can be used, in some cases, for historical and literary purposes.)

Then: "The first and primary duty of government is to protect innocent human life" (Thomas Jefferson). **"Nobody has the freedom to choose to do what's morally wrong" (Abraham Lincoln).**

Now: If the names of all the babies who have been aborted since the early 1970s were placed on a monument (much like that of the *Vietnam Memorial Wall*), it's been estimated that the monument could span over 35 miles. **Although many protest war, very few speak out against abortion. The womb is no longer the safest place, but one of the most dangerous.** What a travesty!

Unbelievable! And we've only touched the tip of the iceberg. (To review more quotes from American history, visit the section entitled *Wisdom Worth Repeating*.) It's extremely disheartening to see how far we have drifted. Clearly, most of America's founders and early settlers wanted the Bible, prayer, and biblical principles so entrenched within society that nothing would remove them. This is why John Adams, one of the signers of the *Declaration of Independence*, rightly said, "The general principles on which the fathers achieved independence were . . . the general principles of Christianity."[17]

The list could go on and on: From Harvard to Yale, from the Supreme Court to the local courts and the public school system, historically, the theme remained the same—God's Word was to be the foundation on which America was built! For example, although the home was where the majority of early Americans were educated, the *Boston Latin School* (established in 1636 by Rev. John Cotton), the first school outside the home, taught students the Word of God. In 1647, the *Old Deluder Law* established the first biblically based public schools in America. **The Colonists believed that they could protect their civil liberties by eliminating biblical illiteracy.**

As yet another example, consider the 1642 *Rules and Precepts* of Harvard University founded by Reverend John Harvard: "Let every student be plainly instructed, and earnestly pressed to consider well, the main end of his life and studies is, to know God and Jesus Christ which is eternal life (John 17:3)." The Rules continue, "and therefore to lay Christ in the bottom, as the only foundation of all sound knowledge and learning." What would those at Harvard say today?

Additionally, one can simply review *The Works of John Witherspoon* to get a glimpse into the biblical mindset of many of the Founders. Reverend Witherspoon, one of the signers of the *Declaration of Independence*, achieved a great reputation as an educator and a religious leader. He is known as "the man who trained the Founding Fathers."

I'm not suggesting that the Founders were without fault, or that they were all Christians; they were human and made mistakes, but in general, most were committed to God's wisdom when they set forth the foundation for government, and ultimately, the nation. A brief review of their *last wills and testaments* will confirm this. It's amazing to see how many of these men acknowledged God and their Savior, Jesus Christ. Additionally, the Founders introduced approximately 1,400 official prayer proclamations prior to 1815. (At some point, the issue of slavery often arises, and rightly so; it was, and is, a formidable mark on our nation's history. However, many Founders were opposed to slavery and diligently fought for abolition. It's important to note some of them—see Appendix II.)

Patrick Henry, an American orator and statesman, and a leading patriot of the American Revolution, is often credited with saying, **"It cannot be emphasized too strongly or too often that this great nation was founded, not by religionists, but by Christians; not on religions, but on the gospel of Jesus Christ."**[18] This is why 24 of the 56 signers of the *Declaration of Independence* received what, today, would be considered a seminary education. This also explains why the Supreme Court, in the early 1800s, ruled that public schools should teach the Bible.[19] **Noah Webster went so far as to say that "education is useless without the Bible."**

History, as well as the original intent of the Founders, does not allow us to separate God's Word from governing our nation. The Founders chose a republic over a democracy for this very reason. A democracy governs by direct vote of the majority of the people; principle-centered leadership was to govern America's republic. Representatives were to vote and administrate according to unchanging biblical principles, not by feelings or opinion polls. Murder, stealing, lying, and so forth are always wrong regardless of how the majority may vote. This isn't a popular stance, or an easy one, but it's the right one! We need more people in leadership who recognize the urgent need to return to biblical principles.

Unlike today, many early political leaders were not ashamed to admit the true source of America's strength—they were biblically correct, rather than politically correct. *They were statesmen, not politicians. A politician thinks of the next election; a statesman thinks of the next generation.* Can you imagine politicians truly acknowledging Jesus today; it would be unheard of. Granted, there are a few, and I thank them for their stance.

> MANY EARLY POLITICAL LEADERS WERE NOT ASHAMED TO ADMIT THE TRUE SOURCE OF AMERICA'S STRENGTH—THEY WERE BIBLICALLY CORRECT, RATHER THAN POLITICALLY CORRECT.

You may wonder, "Where is he going with this?" Straight to the point: Think of what this will mean to our children and grandchildren. **If we fail to stand up for what is right—right now, we may see a time in our history when our freedoms, and theirs, will vanish. With the acceptance of same-sex marriage and failure to protect the unborn, that time may be close at hand.** Psalm 11:3 states, "If the foundations are destroyed, what can the righteous do?" And the last half of Isaiah 7:9 affirms, *If you do not stand firm in your faith and convictions, you will not be able stand at all.* Again, this battle is for the very soul of our nation. It's our choice—will we stand or fall?

GROUP
STUDY QUESTIONS

1. After years of research, the U.S. Supreme Court made this proclamation in 1892: "From the discovery of this continent to the present hour, there is a single voice making this affirmation . . . that this is a Christian nation." Is this significant for us today? Why?

2. What does this statement say about the beliefs of early Americans: History reveals that if a proposed article for the Constitution was not supported by, or rooted in the Bible, it was not considered?

3. In their early writings, many of the Founding Fathers quoted or referenced the Bible nearly four times more than any other source. Why is this noteworthy?

4. Is it significant that 24 of the 56 signers of the *Declaration of Independence* received what, today, would be considered a seminary education? Elaborate.

5. The Courts ruled in the early 1800s that public schools should teach the Bible? Why was this important? Do you agree with the Court's decision?

6. What is the difference between a republican democracy and a true democracy? Why did the Founders choose a republic over a democracy?

7. How can politicians, as well as other Americans, strive to be biblically correct rather than politically correct? List examples.

RESPONSE

1. _____
_____
_____

2. _____
_____
_____

3. _____
_____
_____

4. _____
_____
_____

5. _____
_____
_____

6. _____
_____
_____

7. _____
_____
_____

"Blessed is the nation whose God is the LORD"
(Psalm 33:12).

Recommended Resources

The Christian Life and Character of the Civil Institutions of the United States, by Benjamin F. Morris, was first published in 1864. This remarkable resource contains more than 1,000 pages of original source material making the case that America was founded as a Christian nation, and that early Americans understood the biblical significance of civil government.

Original Intent, by David Barton, brilliantly documents the Founders' own words in relation to forming America's system of government. *The Question of Freemasonry and the Founding Fathers* is another helpful resource from Mr. Barton; it dispels the myth that the Framers were influenced by Freemasonry.

God, Man, and the Law: The Biblical Principles, by Herbert W. Titus, explains how, and to what extent, the Bible has influenced the formation of American law.

Setting the Record Straight: American History in Black & White, from WallBuilders, provides a unique view of the religious and moral heritage of African Americans intertwined with stories from our rich African American political history.

REFLECTION & JOURNALING

Date _____

Additional Thoughts & Chapter Highlights

_____

_____

_____

_____

_____

_____

_____

_____

_____

_____

_____

Prayers & Practical Application

_____

_____

_____

_____

_____

_____

_____

_____

_____

_____

_____

_____

"The church must be reminded that it is not the master or the servant of the state, but rather the conscience of the state."

—MARTIN LUTHER KING, JR. (1929-1968)
Recognized Leader of the Civil Rights Movement;
From his book: *Strength to Love*

FOUR

Shall Congress Prevent Religious Expression?

WITH EXTENSIVE EVIDENCE supporting America's Christian heritage, why do so many deny it? Those who challenge America's history often acquire their information from "revisionists," or from "secular interpretations" concerning what the Founders believed, rather than looking to the Framers' "original" writings. **Revisionists often use omissions, broad generalizations, and half-truths in order to rewrite history.** From slavery to the Salem Witch Trials, from the massacre of Native Americans to the oppression of women, revisionists attempt to level these charges against all early Americans—to take the exception and portray it as the rule. But they often fail to mention the three Christian men who eventually brought an end to the Salem Witch Trials, the countless early Americans who embraced the Indians, and the plethora of Founders who detested the evil practice of slavery. Many early Americans set in motion social movements that have freed and benefited mankind. Granted, some Christians have been guilty of revisionism as well, but the general push toward revisionism often comes from those who feel disdain toward our nation's heritage and anything "Christian."

As yet another example, revisionists try to convince us that people like George Washington were Deists. A Deist believes in an impersonal, distant God; they reject personal prayer, Jesus Christ, and the Bible. Washington used the name "Jesus Christ" in some of his letters, journals, and prayer books; that doesn't sound like a Deist to me. But the most convincing evidence comes from Washington's adopted daughter, Nelly Custis-Lewis: "I should have thought it the greatest heresy to doubt his [George Washington's] firm belief in Christianity. His life, his writings, prove that he was a Christian."[20] If Washington's own contemporaries did not question his faith but were thoroughly convinced of it, should we challenge this fact? (For those who desire more information on this subject, refer to Dr. Peter Lillback's book, *George Washington's Sacred Fire*. This resource buries, under an avalanche of facts, the myth that Washington was an unbeliever.)

Others, however, reject America's heritage because they reject God. Simply stated:

THOSE WHO CRY "SEPARATION OF CHURCH AND STATE" THE LOUDEST ARE OFTEN THOSE WHO REJECT GOD AND HIS PRINCIPLES—THEY WANT THE FREEDOM TO DO WHAT THEY WANT, WHEN THEY WANT, HOW THEY WANT, TO WHOM THEY WANT.

If there's a God, and there is, then the current direction of America's morality is wrong; something few want to admit. This is why many want a complete separation of church and state: Out of sight, out of mind. Those who cry "separation of church and state" the loudest are often those who reject God and His principles—they want the freedom to do what they want, when they want, how they want, to whom they want. I'm not referring to those who desire a healthy debate and/or may disagree with my position—some of the Puritans, for example, preferred a State Church—I'm referring to those who make their own rules and avoid any mention of God. *The arrogant man does not seek God; God is in none of his thoughts* (Psalm 10:4).

A monumental debate about the government's role concerning religion has been ongoing in recent years. For those who understand the foundation on which the Constitution was constructed, there really is no debate. Don't worry, this shouldn't bore you; I'll get straight to the point.

The misconception primarily surrounds the phrase "separation of church and state." Although the First Amendment clearly says that *Congress shall **not** prevent religious expression,* one would think that it reads: *Congress shall prevent religious expression.* The courts have used the infamous "separation" phrase to ban religious activities, primarily those promoting Christian principles. Sadly, many believe that "separation of church and state" appears in the Constitution, when, in reality, the phrase does not appear anywhere in the Constitution. Did you catch that? "Separation of church and state" does **not** appear in the Constitution. So where did it originate? Be very clear on this point, especially if you are a student in a public school or university, or even a "Christian" university. Thomas Jefferson, author of the *Declaration of Independence*, used the phrase in 1802 in a **private letter** written to the Baptist Association of Danbury, Connecticut.[21]

The Baptists feared that the government might someday try to regulate religious expression. Ironically, we are seeing this today. Remember, that's one reason why the Pilgrims left England for Holland before coming to America. This is crucial in understanding the spirit in which the First Amendment was written. **In other words, the Colonists, like the Pilgrims, did not want the government imposing a national religion or denomination on the people— they wanted to worship freely.** Mr. Jefferson wisely agreed with them, as did many of the other Founders.

Jefferson assured the Baptists that the primary purpose of the First Amendment was to prevent rivalry among Christian denominations. He said that Congress would neither establish a national denomination, nor prohibit the free exercise of religion. His statement was intended to **protect** religious expression by building *a wall of separation between the church and the state;* solidifying the fact that the federal government could not strike down religious freedoms.

The first part of the First Amendment reads, "Congress shall make no law respecting an establishment of religion, or prohibiting the free exercise thereof." Note the words, "no law respecting an establishment of religion." The government cannot *establish* a national religion, but it can openly and unapologetically acknowledge the sovereign hand of God. Acknowledgment is not establishment. That's why arguments

> THE GOVERNMENT CANNOT *ESTABLISH* A NATIONAL RELIGION, BUT IT CAN OPENLY AND UNAPOLOGETICALLY *ACKNOWLEDGE* THE SOVEREIGN HAND OF GOD. ACKNOWLEDGMENT IS NOT ESTABLISHMENT.

such as "if you display the Ten Commandments you should also be required to display an alternative message," are absurd. **Ten Commandment monuments can be displayed and prayer can be honored in government offices and in schools without offering alternative messages.** We can openly acknowledge God in all areas of civil government because our government was built on His Word, His precepts, and His principles—we must acknowledge Him as the source of our nation's strength. If you doubt this, simply review the *Annals of Congress* from June 8th to September 25th, 1789. These Annals contain the official records of those who drafted the First Amendment. These gentlemen definitely had something to say about the issue. The delegate from Massachusetts actually said that the First Amendment would read better if it said, "no religious doctrine shall be established by law."

Jefferson said that the freedom to express religion was a God-given right. **The federal government was to be restrained in the area of religion; they could not seize power from the states.** However, approximately 150 years later, in 1947, the Supreme Court radically changed the meaning of the First Amendment. In *Everson v. Board of Education*, the Court did something unheard of: They coupled the First Amendment with the Fourteenth Amendment.

They said that the states could no longer engage in religious activities, and that the federal courts could now restrict such activities. This is clearly opposed to the freedom the Framers envisioned. The state and the church were to be separate in their duties and functions, but interwoven in their core beliefs and principles. In the Old Testament, in the Hebrew Republic, for example, God separated the church from the state in relation to these duties and functions. *The state was to protect, administer justice, and defend the nation. The church was to care for the people, guard the Word of God, and serve as the conscience of the government and the people.* You may want to commit those last few sentences to memory; with that understanding, there's really no debate.

> THE STATE AND THE CHURCH WERE TO BE SEPARATE IN THEIR DUTIES AND FUNCTIONS, BUT INTERWOVEN IN THEIR CORE BELIEFS AND PRINCIPLES.

Remember, this is not about exalting the Founders, America, or the Constitution; it's about promoting godly principles necessary to properly govern the nation.

Just how serious is this issue? In a newsletter entitled, *Truth & Tyranny,* Coral Ridge Ministries made this powerful statement in 2003: "Church-state separation is a lie, and it is deadly. It was this lie that led the Warren Court to ban prayer in public schools in 1962. That ruling set in motion the speediest and most spectacular decline of any civilization in history."[22] Does this statement seem too radical? If so, consider this: It's been estimated that talking, chewing gum, and making noise were the top three public school problems in the early sixties. Some argue that sexual misconduct, robbery, and assault lead the list today. You be the judge.

It's important to note that for 150 years before the 1947 decision, the states had their own powers and rights, and the federal government could not infringe upon them. Religious expression, especially of the Christian faith, was commonly shared. As a matter of fact, many of the original thirteen states had "establishments of religion" known as state-supported churches. Today, however, the courts have taken it upon themselves to assume the role of a law-making body, rather than a protector of the Constitution. **The wall that was designed to protect America's freedoms has now imprisoned her.** It is critical that we pray for our leaders—executive, legislative, and judicial.

Without a doubt, the original intent of many of the Founders was not to remove God's Word from society, but to promote it. An important relationship between *wording* and *intent* must be recognized. Wording divorced from intent leads to speculation. **Many can manipulate the words of early Americans to fit their ideology, but it's difficult to manipulate their intent.** *Intentions clearly indicated that early Americans were concerned about the government influencing religion rather than religion influencing the government.*

FREEDOM *OF* RELIGION WAS NOT FREEDOM *FROM* RELIGION— SEPARATION OF CHURCH AND STATE DOES NOT MEAN SEPARATION OF GOD AND GOVERNMENT.

Freedom *of* religion was not freedom *from* religion—separation of church and state does not mean separation of God and government. National policy was to be shaped by God's principles. For example, many of the ideas found in the *Declaration of Independence* came directly from John Locke's masterful work, *Two Treatises on Civil Government*. In order to illustrate the proper function of civil government, Locke cited the Bible approximately 1,500 times. Additionally, America's three branches of government can be found in Isaiah 33:22, the tax-exempt status for churches in Ezra 7:24, and the reason behind "separation of powers" in Jeremiah 17:9.

Freedom of speech is another misapplied freedom that has cost us dearly. Again, it's important to consider the

> AMERICA'S THREE BRANCHES OF GOVERNMENT CAN BE FOUND IN ISAIAH 33:22, THE TAX-EXEMPT STATUS FOR CHURCHES IN EZRA 7:24, AND THE REASON BEHIND "SEPARATION OF POWERS" IN JEREMIAH 17:9.

words and the intent of the Founders. The infamous *Freedom of Speech* clause was never intended to lead to the distribution of pornographic material, crude dialogue in the media, and an array of other misapplications. **To fully understand the true meaning of freedom of speech, it must be read in context; it deals primarily with protecting religious expression, not protecting offensive material.** I'm not advocating censorship, but there should be a balance between freedom and responsibility; a balance that many have traditionally recognized and respected. James Kent, one of the fathers of *American Jurisprudence* wrote the following in his classic work, *Commentaries on American Law:* "Every citizen might freely speak, write, and print, on any subject, but is responsible for the abuse of that liberty."

If you doubt this, consider the following fact: Many of the early justices participated in drafting the Constitution. One can simply review their rulings in the courtroom to understand how they felt about issues such as "freedom of speech"—rulings reflected convictions. For example, in *The People v. Ruggles* (1811), the defendant was tried in court for making vulgar comments about Jesus and His mother. The defendant's attorney believed that he had an open and shut case, and that his client would not be convicted based on "freedom of speech." The judge, however, did not agree because he understood the true intent of the First Amendment. The defendant was convicted, fined, and sentenced to three months in jail. Although foreign to our way of thinking, Judge Kent plainly stated: "Nothing could be more offensive to the virtuous part of the community, or more injurious to the tender morals of the young, than to declare such profanity lawful."[23] This statement would be ridiculed and seem absurd today. **As a nation, we have, without question, lost our moral and spiritual compass.**

Group
Study Questions

1. What is the difference between the "original" writings of the Founders and secular interpretations? What is revisionism? Why is it dangerous, even for Christians, to accept revisionism?

2. Why do many believe that "separation of church and state" appears in the Constitution? How has this misconception influenced the courts?

3. Why did Jefferson assure the people that Congress would neither establish a national denomination nor prohibit the free exercise of religion? Explain this statement: Acknowledgment is not establishment.

4. The state and the church were designed to be separate in their duties and functions, but interwoven in their core beliefs and principles. How is it possible to be separate, yet interwoven?

5. What is the relationship between the *wording* of the Founders and the *intent* of the Founders? Why is it important to consider both?

6. Comment on this statement: Freedom *of* religion is not freedom *from* religion—separation of church and state does not mean separation of God and government.

7. If the primary purpose of *freedom of speech* was to protect religious expression, how, instead, did pornography and other offensive material fall under its protection?

RESPONSE

1. _____
_____
_____

2. _____
_____
_____

3. _____
_____
_____

4. _____
_____
_____

5. _____
_____
_____

6. _____
_____
_____

7. _____
_____
_____

"Blessed is the nation whose God is the LORD"
(Psalm 33:12).

Recommended Resources

The Exhaustive Concordance to the United States Constitution, available through WallBuilders, is a comprehensive concordance that allows quick reference to every word used in the U.S. Constitution arranged by Article, Section, Clause, and sentence.

The Original 13, by William J. Federer, vividly documents the history of religion in America's first thirteen states. Numerous historical documents provide solid evidence for religion's role in America.

Understanding the Constitution, by David Gibbs, Jr. & David Gibbs III, underscores ten points every Christian should know about the United States Constitution.

Wall of Misconception, by Peter Lillback, clearly and powerfully demonstrates that separation of church and state does not mean separation of God from government.

REFLECTION & JOURNALING

Date _____

Additional Thoughts & Chapter Highlights

_____

_____

_____

_____

_____

_____

_____

_____

_____

_____

_____

Prayers & Practical Application

_____

_____

_____

_____

_____

_____

_____

_____

_____

_____

_____

_____

"Of the 22 civilizations that have appeared in history, 19 of them collapsed when they reached the moral state America is in today."

—ARNOLD TOYNBEE (1889 –1975)
British Historian

FIVE

Sinking One Step at a Time

WITHIN THE LAST FEW DECADES, Americans have seen the destruction of the institution of marriage between a man and a woman, the removal of God's Word in several areas, and the aborting of millions of babies. Ironically, many of the men and women who died for our freedoms did not die for what we are becoming today. They understood sacrifice—duty to Country was duty to God. Many gave their lives in order that we would be "one nation under God," not above God. **A Fifth Division graveyard sign in Iwo Jima, Japan, states it well: "When you go home, tell them for us and say, *'For your tomorrows we gave our today.'* "**[24] What a travesty when we fail to honor those who gave their lives for the freedoms we now enjoy.

In the words of Father O'Brien who served in World War II: "It is the soldier, not the reporter, who has given us the freedom of the press. It is the soldier, not the poet, who has given us the freedom of speech. It is the soldier, not the

campus organizer, who gives us the freedom to demonstrate."
O'Brien continues: "It is the soldier who salutes the flag, who
serves beneath the flag, and whose coffin is draped by the
flag, who allows the protester to burn the flag."

*Let's be very clear on this: "A people that values its
privileges above its principles soon loses both" (Dwight D.
Eisenhower).*[25] Historically, we know that God judged those
nations who continually tolerated sin; wrong choices had
devastating consequences.
Arnold Toynbee, who com-
pleted *A Study of History* in
1961, said: "Of the 22 civilizations that have appeared in
history, 19 of them collapsed
when they reached the moral
state America is in today."[26]

> "IT IS THE SOLDIER
> WHO SALUTES THE
> FLAG, WHO SERVES
> BENEATH THE FLAG,
> AND WHOSE COFFIN
> IS DRAPED BY THE
> FLAG, WHO ALLOWS
> THE PROTESTER TO
> BURN THE FLAG."

Historians realize that a
republican democracy, like
ours in America, cannot last
forever. Eventually, there is a collapse due to moral decay and
financial irresponsibility—liberty often leads to abundance;
abundance to complacency; complacency to apathy; apathy
to a loss of freedom. Based on this, where are we today?
**Unfortunately, countless people are confusing
God's patience with His approval.** "Indeed, I tremble
for my country when I reflect that God is just; that His justice
cannot sleep forever" (Thomas Jefferson).[27] C.S. Lewis said,
"The safest road to hell is the gradual one—the gentle slope,
soft underfoot, without sudden turnings, without milestones,
without signposts."[28]

We're often too smart to take large, deliberate plunges, but we're easily enticed to take one step at a time. One year, with summer approaching, I stepped into my in-laws' swimming pool. My immediate reaction to the piercing cold water was to step out, but to avoid embarrassment, I continued down the steps. I stopped when the water reached my knees. After a few minutes, I continued to move slowly down, stopping for brief

> "INDEED, I TREMBLE FOR MY COUNTRY WHEN I REFLECT THAT GOD IS JUST; THAT HIS JUSTICE CANNOT SLEEP FOREVER"
>
> (THOMAS JEFFERSON).

periods until I was fully submerged. Each step was shocking, but I gradually became comfortable with the cold water—my body accepted what was initially shocking. In the same way, we've become comfortable with sin, and what once alarmed us now amuses us. We continue to hear: "Come on in, it's not that bad, everyone is doing it!" And we step right in. **America has been desensitized one generation at a time, one court decision at a time, one compromise at a time, and we are drowning in a cesspool of relativism.** *The wicked freely parade and prance about while evil is praised throughout the land* (Psalm 12:8).

As I said earlier, there are times to encourage, motivate, and uplift, but there are also times to confront, challenge, and contend for what is right—that time is now! We are experiencing the rapid deterioration of a nation right before our eyes. This is not the time for passivity, but for change. We've heard these questions before, and we will hear them again: If not now, when? If not here, where? If not us, who?

God said that He looked for a man from among the leaders who would build a wall and stand in the gap before Him on behalf of the land that He might not destroy it . . . (Ezekiel 22:30). This was true in Ezekiel's day, and it's true today. We are sinking one step at a time, but God is still looking for good men and women to do what is right.

This is a difficult message, I know, but I make no apologies. *In this case, when we fail to confront, we confirm.* **When we fail to confront destructive ideas and philosophies, we are, in essence, confirming them. We cannot change what we will not confront; we must speak the truth in love.**

"Speaking the truth in love" reminds me of an experience I had with my daughter, Aubrey, when she was 18 months old. My wife and I had the opportunity to take her to a small feline zoo. As we walked through the facility we saw leopards, tigers, and other exotic felines; my daughter enjoyed seeing all the "kitty cats." Before leaving, we took a ride on a miniature train. As we rounded the first turn, I was amazed and shocked to see a larger than life, full-size lion leaning against the chain-link as his massive paws slammed against the fence.

As the train moved slowly through the lion exhibit, I looked down, and to my horror, my daughter was unbuckling her seat belt. She shouted, "Daddy, hug the lion; play with the lion," as she desperately tried to get out of the train. I replied with an emphatic, "No," as I pulled her tightly to me and refastened her seat belt. Needless to say, she wasn't happy. She began crying, hoping that it would change my mind. To her, and others looking on from a distance, I may have appeared narrow-minded, judgmental, and intolerant, but had I let my daughter play with the lion she could have been mauled to death. That's the truth in love—loving someone enough to tell him or her the truth, even if it hurts. If being labeled narrow-minded, judgmental, and intolerant is the cost of speaking the truth in love, so be it. If we know there is a roaring lion waiting to devour, we should lovingly speak the truth.

For those who say, "I don't want to get involved," we must remember that we're already involved—by saying nothing we say something. Our government is a government of the people, by the people, for the people. This means that a believer should be involved in running for office, voting, and/or monitoring those in office to assure that they perform their duties. The welfare of society often falls in the hands of the Christian community. For those who believe we should remain passive and silent, I challenge you to read the writings of the Old Testament prophets. They lamented, shed tears, and pleaded with the people and the leaders to turn from their sins and to turn back to God—they spoke the truth in love. Even Jesus wept for Jerusalem when He saw that her destruction was near.

The same cry goes out today in America where we increase our wealth, but decrease our values. We search the heavens for the answers, but turn from the One who created them. We call ourselves a "Christian nation," but we often reject the biblical principles that made America great. Sadly, we call this progress. Martin Luther King, Jr., in a letter from Birmingham Jail on April 16, 1963, wrote, "We will have to repent in this generation not merely for the hateful words and actions of the bad people but for the appalling silence of the good people." I hold the same opinion today.

GROUP
STUDY QUESTIONS

1. What might the Framers have added to the Constitution (to clarify their position) had they foreseen the destruction of the institution of marriage between a man and a woman, and the aborting of millions of babies?

2. Is this statement from World War II significant for us today: *"When you go home, tell them for us and say, 'For your tomorrows we gave our today' "*? Explain.

3. Explain Dwight D. Eisenhower's statement: "A people that values its privileges above its principles soon loses both."

4. Do you believe that many Americans are confusing God's patience with His approval? If so, give examples.

5. Do you agree that America has been desensitized one generation at a time, one court decision at a time, one compromise at a time, and that we are submerged in a cesspool of relativism? List some examples.

6. Can we call ourselves a "Christian nation" while at the same time reject the biblical principles that made America great? Explain your position.

7. How do Martin Luther King, Jr.'s words apply to us today: "We will have to repent in this generation not merely for the hateful words and actions of the bad people but for the appalling silence of the good people"?

Response

1. _____
   _____
   _____

2. _____
   _____
   _____

3. _____
   _____
   _____

4. _____
   _____
   _____

5. _____
   _____
   _____

6. _____
   _____
   _____

7. _____
   _____
   _____

"Blessed is the nation whose God is the LORD"
(Psalm 33:12).

RECOMMENDED RESOURCES

The Spirit of the American Revolution, available through WallBuilders, is a small booklet that reveals the motivation behind the American Revolution.

So Help Me God, by Roy Moore (former Chief Justice of the Supreme Court of Alabama), describes the providential events in his life leading up to his removal from office. He also offers a thorough explanation of the true "rule of law," and why America is losing ground one court decision at a time.

The League of Grateful Sons, from Vision Forum Ministries, documents the godly legacy of the fathers of World War II. It provides a glimpse into the spirit of America as seen through the eyes of those who defended our nation. (DVD, 75 minutes.) I also recommend the video curriculum from Vision Forum adapted from the Witherspoon School of Law and Public Policy entitled: Introduction to Christianity, Law, and Culture.

A Nation Adrift: Standing at the Crossroads of America's Destiny, from American Vision, is a fact-packed documentary on America's Christian history. It is replete with quotations from many of our Founding Fathers and notable figures from history. (DVD, 90 minutes.)

Reflection & Journaling

Date _____

Additional Thoughts & Chapter Highlights

_____
_____
_____
_____
_____
_____
_____
_____
_____
_____
_____
_____

Prayers & Practical Application

_____
_____
_____
_____
_____
_____
_____
_____
_____
_____
_____
_____
_____
_____

"The law . . . dictated by God Himself is, of course, superior in obligation to any other. It is binding over all the globe, in all countries, and at all times. No human laws are of any validity if contrary to this."[29]

—ALEXANDER HAMILTON (1755– 1804)
Signer of the Constitution

SIX

Religion and Politics— Do They Mix?

ONE OF THE MOST CONTROVERSIAL ISSUES of our time is the question of mixing religion and politics. One group believes that the church should be used as a political platform, the other advocates passivity. So, what's the answer?

First and foremost, we cannot deny our primary responsibility: To encourage people to turn to Christ as their Lord and Savior. This is how America will "truly" change from the inside out. The No. 1 problem in America is not a political problem; it's a spiritual problem called sin. **The primary goal of the church is not to become a political movement, but a spiritual influence.** Christianity has influenced large-scale changes because it first transformed the hearts of men and women.

Politics won't save America anymore than a dumbbell will save someone who is drowning; however, we cannot

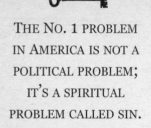

THE NO. 1 PROBLEM IN AMERICA IS NOT A POLITICAL PROBLEM; IT'S A SPIRITUAL PROBLEM CALLED SIN.

ignore our God-given civic responsibility and the massive impact that politics has on our society. Make no mistake about it: America's leaders play an enormous role in shaping the direction of the country. "When the righteous are in authority, the people rejoice; but when the wicked man rules, the people groan" (Proverbs 29:2). For instance, there are legislators who support partial-birth abortion, even when the life of the mother is not at risk. Partial-birth abortion is a process where an unborn, often healthy, baby's body is delivered feet first, often near full term, until only the head remains inside the womb. (The head remains in the womb so that the abortion is not considered murder. Once a baby is fully delivered, his/her life cannot be terminated.) The physician then punctures the back of the child's skull with a sharp instrument and removes the child's brains before delivering the dead baby.

There are also those who support D & E (dilation and evacuation) abortions and saline abortions. During a D & E abortion, a large crushing instrument is inserted into the uterus. The physician grabs the baby with this instrument and pulls off pieces (limbs) until he or she is completely removed from the mother. During a saline abortion, a salt solution is injected into the mother's sac for the baby to swallow. Once swallowed, the baby begins to experience a violent, slow death—so violent that the mother can actually feel the baby in her womb fighting for his or her life.

These paragraphs were extremely difficult for me to write—I shed many tears, contemplated removing them, and prayed diligently for direction. But I cannot, and will not, remain silent. **There is a reason why "mother," "baby," and "abort" have been changed to "a woman's right to choose"; it's a marketing ploy designed to hide a brutal practice.** Abortion is a travesty and our nation has the blood of innocent children on her hands.

It's been estimated that approximately four hundred of these types of abortions are performed every day in America after the third month of pregnancy. We can no longer remain silent while silent screams go unheard. When medical professionals can look into a trash can full of mutilated babies after a day's worth of abortions and see nothing wrong with this, their consciences have been seared. **When human life is devalued, atrocities such as the Holocaust, the slave trade, and abortion occur. God help us when we destroy what He has created.**

Fortunately, at the time of this writing, the Supreme Court ruled against pro-choice legislators and upheld the ban on the grizzly form of abortion known as partial-birth abortion, yet there are still those in leadership who disagree with the Court's decision and who allow D & E and saline abortions to continue. This is a shame to

PSALM 139:13...*GOD FORMED MY INWARD PARTS; HE KNIT ME TOGETHER IN MY MOTHER'S WOMB.* ON THE ISSUE OF ABORTION, THERE IS ONLY ONE POSITION— GOD'S POSITION.

America, and a mockery before God who said, "Before I formed you in the womb I knew you" (Jeremiah 1:5). Psalm 139:13 says that *God formed my inward parts; He knit me together in my mother's womb.* On the issue of abortion, there is only one position—God's position. But there is hope for those who have participated in, or who have had an abortion. If this is you, I encourage you to read chapter eight, as well as Psalm 51. Both personal experience and the Bible have taught me that God's unfailing love and compassion will see you through.

On the other hand, politics has been instrumental in movements to protect the unborn and the poor, as well as the abolition of slavery, women's rights, and the Civil Rights Movement, to mention only a few. These events all transpired because Christians took action. Recall what was said earlier: *God looked for a man from among the **leaders** who would stand in the gap and intercede for the land.* Leadership matters!

In the realm of government, there are two primary areas of responsibility for us to consider. One is God's eternal kingdom; the other is the world's political system. We have a responsibility to both, and God's eternal principles establish the foundation for both. Our political system, ordained by God, oversees the affairs of men. The primary role of government is to secure our God-given rights. Remember: The state and the church are to be separate in their duties and functions, but interwoven in their core beliefs and principles. The institution of government was created by God to govern man—to protect and defend, and to administer justice. This is why it's unwise to apply, as some do, many of Jesus' teachings such as, "turning the other cheek," to the institution of government. Contextually, Jesus was referring to personal affronts and insults, not to the administration of justice.

One of the primary purposes of government is to protect those who obey the law from those who break it. **And this sometimes refers to war.** Although war is detestable, it may be necessary to restrain evil. (Refer to Romans 13:1-7.)

The question often arises then, "Can we legislate morality?" No and yes. No, we cannot change a person's heart by forcing a set of laws or rules upon them, but we can restrain evil and deter wrongdoing. *We should all strive to defend the weak*

> "NOW, MORE THAN EVER BEFORE, THE PEOPLE ARE RESPONSIBLE FOR THE CHARACTER OF THEIR CONGRESS. IF THAT BODY BE IGNORANT, RECKLESS, AND CORRUPT, IT IS BECAUSE THE PEOPLE TOLERATE IGNORANCE, RECKLESSNESS, AND CORRUPTION."
>
> JAMES A. GARFIELD, TWENTIETH PRESIDENT OF THE UNITED STATES

and the fatherless, maintain the rights of the poor and oppressed, and deliver them from the hand of the wicked (Psalm 82:3-4). Most laws are connected to some type of moral system—the laws of a nation establish the foundation. The government cannot remain neutral, or separate, from the foundation on which it rests. Granted, many governments, including our own, often fall short; that's why we should strive to be on God's side rather than always assuming that He is on ours. God ordained the institution of government, but He does not approve of every form of government. Nevertheless, it's important to recognize the significance of the institution of government and to respect its authority.

Second, we should not overlook our civic responsibilities as Christians—if a mere 50 percent of eligible Christian voters would vote, the political landscape would change dramatically. James A. Garfield, an ordained minister and twentieth President of the United States, said, "Now, more than ever before, the people are responsible for the character of their Congress. If that body be ignorant, reckless, and corrupt, it is because the people tolerate ignorance, recklessness, and corruption."

> "WE'RE NOT JUST TALKING ABOUT ADDING MILLIONS OF DOLLARS TO THE NATIONAL DEFICIT; WE'RE TALKING ABOUT ABORTING MILLIONS OF BABIES. WE'RE NOT ONLY TALKING ABOUT FLUCTUATIONS IN THE HOUSING MARKET; WE'RE TALKING ABOUT CREATING LIFE SIMPLY TO DESTROY IT. THIS SHIFT REQUIRES US TO STAY CLOSELY INVOLVED.

We don't have to abandon our ethics or compromise our principles to be involved in politics—what good is salt left in the shaker, or a light that is hidden? Contextually, when Jesus referred to being the "salt and light," He was referring to holy living at the individual level, but the overlapping principle applies to all areas of life. *"Politics" is not a bad word. In simple terms, politics refers to governing or leading a group of people.* Again, politics won't save America, but in order to implement change and help others, we must take action; hence the political process.

Politics that once focused largely on the economy, national security, and the deficit, now tackles important moral issues.

These major issues have enormous implications; to remain silent actually makes a statement that we are not concerned enough. This is not just about the loss of jobs; it's about the loss of morality. We're not just talking about adding millions of dollars to the national deficit; we're talking about aborting millions of babies. We're not only talking about fluctuations in the housing market; we're talking about creating life simply to destroy it. This shift requires us to stay closely involved. Topics that are "too controversial" are often critically important; we can no longer ignore them.

Unfortunately, we forget that apathy today will be our downfall tomorrow. Recall the words of Martin Luther King, Jr., "The church must be reminded that it is not the master or the servant of the state, but rather the conscience of the state." He continues, "If the church does not recapture its prophetic zeal, it will become an irrelevant social club without moral or spiritual authority." What an insightful perspective, especially for us today.

The short answer to the question, "Can we mix religion and politics?" is yes—separate but interwoven. Government and religion should not "sleep in the same bed" so to speak. **The government has distinct and separate responsibilities from the church; abuses can occur under a State Church form of government; most students of history realize this.** On the other hand, leaders must lead according to unchanging biblical truths found in God's Word. Although this Scripture was intended for the nation of Israel, the principle can still apply to us today: *If you diligently obey the voice of the LORD and observe all that He has commanded you, He will set you high above all the nations of the earth* (Deuteronomy 28:1). Religion and politics must work together.

GROUP
STUDY QUESTIONS

1. Explain the controversy, as well as your opinion, concerning mixing religion and politics. Do you believe that the prevailing problem in America is a spiritual problem? Why? Why not?

2. What are your thoughts on abortion in light of these Scriptures: Jeremiah 1:5, Psalm 139:13, Proverbs 6:16-17, and Deuteronomy 5:17?

3. How can we make every effort to be on God's side rather than always assuming that He is on our side? List a few practical ways.

4. In the realm of government, there are two areas of responsibility—God's eternal kingdom and the world's political system. How can we be instrumental in both?

5. Can we legislate morality? Can a government remain neutral in writing and enforcing law? Explain your position.

6. Today, we're not just talking about the national deficit, or the housing market; we're talking about aborting millions of babies, and creating life simply to destroy it. Does this shift require us to stay closely involved? Explain.

7. What distinct and separate responsibilities does the government have from the church? And vice versa?

RESPONSE

1. _____
_____
_____

2. _____
_____
_____

3. _____
_____
_____

4. _____
_____
_____

5. _____
_____
_____

6. _____
_____
_____

7. _____
_____
_____

"Blessed is the nation whose God is the LORD"
(Psalm 33:12).

RECOMMENDED RESOURCES

The New-England Primer, introduced in 1690 by Benjamin Harris, was the first textbook printed in America. Many early Americans learned to read from this simple, yet effective book. It was the beginning textbook for students when religion and education went hand in hand.

Lives of the Signers of the Declaration of Independence, originally published in 1848 by Benson J. Lossing, is a brief biography of each of the signers. This resource reveals that early Americans understood the wisdom in allowing religion and politics to work together.

A Testament of Hope—The Essential Writings and Speeches of Martin Luther King, Jr., published by Harper Collins, unveils the man behind the movement, and how his religious convictions led to the Civil Rights Movement.

America's God and Country, by William J. Federer, is an encyclopedia of quotations from founders, presidents, statesmen, courts, scientists, etc. This helpful resource reinforces the fact that America was built on religious expression—in public as well as in private.

REFLECTION & JOURNALING

Date _____

Additional Thoughts & Chapter Highlights

_____
_____
_____
_____
_____
_____
_____
_____
_____
_____
_____

Prayers & Practical Application

_____
_____
_____
_____
_____
_____
_____
_____
_____
_____
_____
_____
_____

"The only thing necessary for the triumph of evil is for good men [and women] to do nothing."

—EDMUND BURKE (1729-1797)
Author, Orator, and Political Theorist

SEVEN

Why Didn't Someone Do Something?

FIVE WORDS STILL HAUNT MY THOUGHTS TODAY. Sometime ago, I sat speechless as I listened to a man recount his trip to a Holocaust museum with his young daughter. As they walked by photos of the death camps, gas chambers, and countless bodies piled one upon another, his daughter silently contemplated the horrors that were unfolding before her eyes.

When the tour ended, they drove home without saying a word. The father wondered if she truly understood the significance of the event. Was she too young to view such depravity? Was she too fragile to cope with the truth of the Holocaust? Would it make a negative impact on her life? Would it leave her fearful and wounded? Would she begin to doubt God?

His questions were answered nearly two hours later when his daughter finally spoke. She looked at her father and asked, "Daddy, why didn't someone do something?"

Will we hear those same haunting words from our children and grandchildren? Yes! If we fail to contend for what is right, we may see a time in our history when our children will ask, "Why didn't someone do something?" Sadly, we may not be able to answer.

What can I do? What can we do? People are often willing to help, but they lack motivation; they also don't know where to begin. How can we honor God and preserve our values? Here are just a few ways:

1. **Lead a life of integrity regardless of what society promotes.** Although only a select few can change government policy, all of us can build a life of moral integrity while staying committed to God's Word. Certain "rights" and "wrongs" called absolutes are given by God to save man from himself. One of the best ways to make a difference is to live a life based on moral absolutes, and by letting

> CERTAIN "RIGHTS" AND "WRONGS" CALLED ABSOLUTES ARE GIVEN BY GOD TO SAVE MAN FROM HIMSELF.

honesty and integrity guide our decisions. Again, society changes as individuals change.

M.H. McKee states it well, **"Integrity is one of several paths. It distinguishes itself from the others because it is the right path, and the only one upon which you will never get lost."** Proverbs 11:3 adds, "The integrity of the upright will guide them."

Combine integrity, wisdom, Scripture study, counsel, and prayer, and you'll have a better grasp on what

God is calling you to do. Unfortunately, we want to hear from God first and work on character later, but God wants us to work on character first—we'll then be better able to hear. A life of moral excellence and integrity leads to a growing

> **PRAYER IS MORE POWERFUL THAN PROTEST! WE SHOULD NOT RELY ON POLITICAL POWER, BUT ON THE POWER OF GOD THROUGH PRAYER.**

relationship with God. (See 2 Peter 1:5.)

2. **Pray and fast for our nation.** Prayer is more powerful than protest! We should not rely on political power, but on the power of God through prayer. The great preacher, **C.H. Spurgeon, once said, "I would rather teach one man to pray than ten men to preach."**

   For those who doubt the power of prayer in America's history, consider this excerpt from the book, *One Nation Under God—The History of Prayer in America:* "Prayer stands as one of the most critical and indisputable factors to have influenced the course of American history."[30] Many of those who study history understand the connection. (On that note, I recommend Daniel Henderson's book, *Fresh Encounters—Experiencing Transformation Through United Worship-based Prayer.*)

3. **Vote for principles, not a particular party.** "He who rules over men must be just" (2 Samuel 23:3). We need more humble, God-fearing leaders. The Lord hates pride, arrogance, and self-centeredness. Without humility and a teachable spirit, it's difficult, if not impossible, to govern properly. **Humility does not mean that lead-**

ers become passive pawns, but that they live in total surrender to God; they're more concerned with God's opinion than opinion polls. It's been said that the quality of our government depends more upon the character of our leaders than upon our laws. *But be careful—many use "religious talk" and twist the Scriptures to support un-biblical initiatives.* For example, in one setting leaders will express their religious convictions and quote the Bible, but in another setting they'll vote for partial-birth abortion and against protecting babies who survive late-term abortions. Judge what they "do" more than what they "say."

> ○━━═
>
> IT'S BEEN SAID THAT THE QUALITY OF OUR GOVERNMENT DEPENDS MORE UPON THE CHARACTER OF OUR LEADERS THAN UPON OUR LAWS.

Again, we can no longer hide behind the excuse, "I don't want to get involved." As citizens, we are given the privilege, for now, to place people in positions of leadership. *Whether we like it or not, we are involved. Millions are not registered to vote; and millions of registered voters stay at home.* We'll stand in line to see a movie, but we won't stand in line to vote and elect leaders who will affect the direction of our country. This makes a statement about what we value—and isn't it sad.

4. **Become involved, but with the right motives.** Don't initiate or pursue anything with a rebellious, prideful attitude. **You can be right in your reasoning, yet wrong in your attitude.** Anger over issues that anger the Lord, such as crime, abortion, pornography, abuse,

oppression, and so on, is justifiable and can cause positive action. If anger causes damage to another, or personally damages your character, it's probably not accomplishing God's purpose. If anger sparks prayer and a Christlike stance, it can be productive. This may have been why Martin Luther said, "When I am angry, I can pray well and preach well."

William Wilberforce (1759-1833) became very angry over the slave trade in Britain. Wilberforce, a Christian member of parliament, was very influential in the abolition of the slave trade, and eventually slavery itself in the British Empire. When he was deciding whether to enter politics or serve the Lord, John Newton, a former slave ship captain and author of the powerful hymn *Amazing Grace,* gave him wise counsel to do both. Thank God that he did. As it is with us, we can do both if God is calling us to a specific field of interest.

On the other hand, many have been guilty of not getting involved by saying, "We shouldn't say or do anything political. All we need to do is preach the gospel." Be careful . . . although the gospel is our primary focus, this shouldn't be an excuse

WE'LL STAND IN LINE TO SEE A MOVIE, BUT WE WON'T STAND IN LINE TO VOTE AND ELECT LEADERS WHO WILL AFFECT THE DIRECTION OF OUR COUNTRY. THIS MAKES A STATEMENT ABOUT WHAT WE VALUE— AND ISN'T IT SAD.

against action. Charles Finney (1792-1875), a major leader in the *Second Great Awakening,* said, "God cannot sustain this free and blessed country which we love and pray for unless the Church will take right ground." Finney continues, "Politics are a part of religion in such a country as this, and Christians must do their duty to the country as a part of their duty to God."

5. **Engage, not *enrage*, the culture.** Since evangelicals are often viewed as irrational, conceited, narrow-minded, and unintelligent, we need to engage the culture with humility, wisdom, patience, and discernment. Why would God ordain a government such as ours in America and not ask us to be involved? That's why it's important to know both sides of political "hot buttons"—knowledge allows us to make the right decisions.

If you decide to speak out, articulate your message clearly, patiently, and wisely. But always make sure your actions are backed by a clear biblical mandate. Respond; don't react! Abraham Lincoln once suggested, "Better to remain silent and be thought a fool than to speak out and remove all doubt." A reaction often calls for an apology, while a response generally thinks things through, and often, no apologies are needed. However, extreme anger-driven demonstration and protest is often not the answer, neither is a total lack of involvement—there must be a balance. Our goal should not be to come across harsh, overly critical, or arrogant, but to speak the truth from a gentle spirit. Granted, this is hard. Many times, I'd rather forcefully quote Scriptures and end the argument instead of allowing a gentle spirit to guide my words. **Meekness is not the absence of strength; it's strength under control.** *It takes a great deal of strength to engage the culture in a spirit of humility while avoiding being harsh,* *cruel, and insensitive.* A gentle response, underscored with truth, can win far more than a harsh response.

> "LIGHT AND DARKNESS, RIGHT AND WRONG, GOOD AND EVIL, TRUTH AND ERROR ARE INCOMPATIBLES . . . WHEN THEY COMPROMISE IT IS THE LIGHT, THE RIGHT, THE GOOD, AND THE TRUTH THAT ARE DAMAGED"
>
> (W. Graham Scroggie).

Some may argue, "What about Jesus' aggressive approach when He confronted the religious leaders?" First, He was dealing primarily with hypocrisy, not politics. Second, this approach may be the exception from time to time, but never the rule. Third, He knew the heart of those He was confronting—we don't. Remember, you can be right in your reasoning, yet wrong in your attitude. The question shouldn't be, "How can I win this argument?" but rather, "How can I persuasively and patiently articulate my message without compromising my Christian character?"

I thank God for Christians who are involved and who influence America's political climate. I wish there were more who would engage, rather than enrage the culture. I'm not suggesting we compromise our principles or God's Word in the pursuit of peace or unity—"Light and darkness, right and wrong, good and evil, truth and error are incompatibles . . . when they compromise it is the light, the right, the good, and the truth that are damaged" (W. Graham Scroggie). **Truth cannot be compromised— God blesses and honors the peacemaker but not the religious negotiator.** Standing up for truth according to God's Word, will, at times, enrage others; this is not what I'm referring to. I'm referring to those who ignite anger by being obnoxious, vain, conceited, and blatantly disrespectful. Avoid this at all costs.

6. **Recognize diversity.** In my opinion, failure to recognize diverse gifts may explain why many people are divided on the issue of religion and politics. For instance, John MacArthur, James Dobson, Chuck Colson, Chuck Smith, Billy Graham, and D. James Kennedy have/had different ministries, but all fall under the umbrella of Christian service. God creates, within each of us, varying desires, talents, and levels of interests. If God has called a man to preach and teach His Word, that will be his passion. If God has called a Christian to pursue politics, that will be his or her passion, and so on.

> IN MY OPINION, FAILURE TO RECOGNIZE DIVERSE GIFTS MAY EXPLAIN WHY MANY PEOPLE ARE DIVIDED ON THE ISSUE OF RELIGION AND POLITICS.

Problems arise when we become judgmental and fail to respect our differences. Activists should not expect everyone to share their passion for politics, and those who believe Christians should stay out of politics must understand that God clearly calls some Christians to the political arena. God established the concept of government, why would He not desire godly leadership? Granted, there will always be a moral divide in America, but this should not deter us from making a difference. It took years for America to reach this state of moral decay; it may take years to recover.

7. **Expect opposition.** As you begin to make a difference and honor God's Word, expect opposition. The enemy will oppose you through self-doubt, misplaced anger, impatience, and unforgiveness. He'll use pessimistic people and/or fill your mind with negative thoughts in an attempt to discourage you. Those trying to make a difference may be taunted by the thought, "It's useless; why try?" or, "God can't really use me." The enemy emphasizes the negative, but God, not the enemy, oversees the process. *When God is for you, no one can stand against you. God is greater than the challenge that you are facing.*

We should also view challenging situations as opportunities to develop character. The only way to develop qualities such as love, joy, peace, humility, and patience is to be confronted with situations that require love, joy, peace, humility, and patience. How do we develop patience if we're not tested? How do we develop forgiveness if we are never wronged? How do we learn to trust God if we're never in need? **How do we develop character if we are never challenged?**

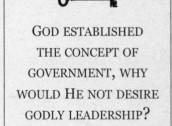

GOD ESTABLISHED THE CONCEPT OF GOVERNMENT, WHY WOULD HE NOT DESIRE GODLY LEADERSHIP?

8. **Never give up.** You can make a difference—we can make a difference. Remember my earlier mention of William Wilberforce? Wilberforce died just three days after hearing of the passage of the *Slavery Abolition Act* in 1833. His efforts to end slavery actually began forty-six years earlier, in 1787, when he met a group of anti-slave trade activists who motivated him to get involved. God

will move mountains on behalf of one committed person, but it often takes time. You might think you are one of only a few in your community who is concerned about doing what is right. Elijah, an Old Testament prophet, felt this way when he cried: *They have torn down Your altars and killed Your prophets, and only I am left. But God responded, I have seven thousand people you do not know about who are still loyal to Me.* (See 1 Kings 19.) **Be encouraged: God simply asks that we do our part while He does His.**

9. **Make a relationship with Christ your top priority.** My father often took me trap shooting throughout my younger years. As soon as the clay target was released, I'd raise my shotgun and fire. I had only seconds to aim and shoot as it darted through the air. If I lost sight of the target, I would miss the shot. The same holds true with making a difference. If we neglect to focus on the target— our personal relationship with Jesus Christ—we can miss the mark: God's most productive plan for our life.

> THE ONLY WAY TO DEVELOP QUALITIES SUCH AS LOVE, JOY, PEACE, HUMILITY, AND PATIENCE IS TO BE CONFRONTED WITH SITUATIONS THAT REQUIRE LOVE, JOY, PEACE, HUMILITY, AND PATIENCE.

As a Southern California corporate executive, I experienced the devastating effects of life in the fast lane without rules or boundaries. To briefly read about how the message of the gospel radically changed my life, refer to *Religion v. Relationship—A Personal Note From the Author,* at the end of this book. With that said, let's end with the final, and most important chapter—*Our Only Hope.*

Group
Study Questions

1. How did the story of the young girl's visit to the Holocaust museum affect you? Will there be a time when our children ask, "Why didn't someone do something?"

2. How important is it to lead a life of integrity regardless of what society promotes? Are there certain "rights" and "wrongs" called absolutes? If so, list examples.

3. Prayer is more powerful than protest. We should not rely on political power, but on the power of God through prayer. Do you agree or disagree? Why?

4. Do you believe we should vote for principles and not necessarily a particular party? Explain your position.

5. Comment on this statement: Don't initiate with a rebellious, prideful attitude. How can you be right in your reasoning, yet wrong in your attitude?

6. How should we engage the culture? How important is humility, wisdom, patience, discernment, and meekness? Give an example of how each one of these character traits should be used.

7. Do you agree that all of us have different God-given abilities, desires, and responsibilities? If so, how does this understanding help you avoid being judgmental?

RESPONSE

1. _____
_____
_____

2. _____
_____
_____

3. _____
_____
_____

4. _____
_____
_____

5. _____
_____
_____

6. _____
_____
_____

7. _____
_____
_____

"Blessed is the nation whose God is the LORD"
(Psalm 33:12).

Recommended Resources

Sinful Silence, by Ken Connor and John Revell, supports civil involvement using biblical principles. This book also discloses some of the pitfalls of remaining silent.

Why You Can't Stay Silent, by Tom Minnery, exposes the power of Christians compelled by God's love to change the course of history.

What if Jesus Had Never Been Born, by D. James Kennedy and Jerry Newcombe, lists many examples of the impact of Christ and Christianity on history.

The Role of Pastors and Christians in Civil Government, by David Barton, shows how the church, and pastors, played an invaluable role in the struggle for America's independence.

REFLECTION & JOURNALING

Date _____

Additional Thoughts & Chapter Highlights

_____
_____
_____
_____
_____
_____
_____
_____
_____
_____
_____

Prayers & Practical Application

_____
_____
_____
_____
_____
_____
_____
_____
_____
_____
_____
_____
_____

"The proud, self-justifying, self-reliant, self-seeking self has to come simply as a lost, undone sinner, whose only hope is a justifying Savior."

—NORMAN GRUBB (1895-1993)
Missionary and Author;
From his book: *Continuous Revival*

EIGHT

Our Only Hope

I looked throughout America to find where her greatness originated. I looked for it in her harbors and on her shorelines, in her fertile fields and boundless prairies, and in her gold mines and vast world commerce, but it was not there. *It was not until I went to the churches of America and heard her pulpits aflame with righteousness did I understand the secret of her success.* America is great because she is good, and if America ceases to be good, America will cease to be great. (Paraphrase)

THIS POWERFUL DECLARATION OFTEN APPEARS in books, speeches, lectures, and sermons. Even though it is not found in his works, it's often attributed to Alexis De Tocqueville—a Frenchman who authored *Democracy in America* in the early 1800s. Whomever the author, it's clear that America's success was attributed to the pulpits being aflame with righteousness. Churches have often served as the moral compass for the nation—to confront, challenge, encourage, and exhort. And this is precisely where I'd like to bring this book to a close.

It's time for us to turn back to absolute truth and away from relativism—back to Christ and away from the broad road that leads to destruction. We must repent, ask for forgiveness, and seek restoration. We should not apologize for preaching God's Word, redefine what He meant, or back down from conflict. We are in the midst of a spiritual battle. We will be hated for following Christ, mocked for believing in truth, and challenged for promoting righteousness. We are called to deny ourselves, pick up our cross, and follow Him. Clearly, the day of the passive church is over. We must lovingly preach righteousness in our pulpits again: "Righteousness exalts a nation, but sin is a reproach to any people" (Proverbs 14:34).

> "THE LORD HAS BEEN SO DEEPLY GRIEVED BY THE REFUSAL OF THE CHURCH TO FAITHFULLY PROCLAIM THE WHOLE COUNSEL OF HIS WORD IN THE POWER OF THE HOLY SPIRIT THAT HE HAS LARGELY WITHDRAWN FROM THE CHURCH AND LEFT HER TO HER OWN DEVICES."
>
> RICHARD OWEN ROBERTS

Richard Owen Roberts said it well, "The Lord has been so deeply grieved by the refusal of the church to faithfully proclaim the whole counsel of His Word in the power of the Holy Spirit that He has largely withdrawn from the church and left her to her own devices." Roberts continues, "The heart cry of God is most certainly, 'Return to Me, and I will return to you.' "[31]

The greatest threat to Christians in America is not false religion, secularism, atheism, or any other "ism," but compromise. **When compromise occurs we avoid the** difficult truths of the Bible and decentralize the Scriptures. We "play" Christian but compromise everything that Christ stood for. We have riches, wealth, and prosperity, but neglect the weightier matters—love, mercy, and forgiveness. When compromise reigns, we can easily become insensitive, indifferent, ineffective, unforgiving, unloving,

> "WHERE DOES CHRISTIANITY DESTROY ITSELF IN A GIVEN GENERATION? IT DESTROYS ITSELF BY NOT LIVING IN THE LIGHT, BY PROFESSING A TRUTH IT DOES NOT OBEY"
>
> (A.W. TOZER).

and self-righteous. "Where does Christianity destroy itself in a given generation? It destroys itself by not living in the light, by professing a truth it does not obey" (A.W. Tozer).

America was great because many of her early leaders understood sacrifice and their need for God; they sincerely repented and turned to Him—they had genuine faith. Genuine faith is reflected in a transformed life, a love for God and His Word, sincere humility, selfless love, and true repentance. **There is always a link between genuine faith and sincere repentance. Change will occur in America when there is a strong conviction of sin, sincere repentance, and genuine faith.** Repentance is not an outdated, irrelevant word; it's a positive word from the heart of God. Jesus, as well as John the Baptist, both began their ministry by proclaiming, "Repent, for the kingdom of heaven is at hand" (Matthew 3:2; 4:17).

Self-improvement is not repentance. Repentance is a change of mind that leads to a change in action—brokenness, genuine sorrow over sin, and humility are all marks of sincere repentance. Many wrongly confuse tears with repentance. It's possible to be sorry, but not repentant. A penitent person sees sin as God sees it and turns from it. They do not want to continue in hurtful or harmful behavior. They accept full responsibility for their actions. At this point, tears often follow, and rightly so. The danger comes when arrogance and a hardness of heart, as we often see today, prevent us from turning to God.

> FOUNDATIONAL DOCTRINES SUCH AS THE CROSS, SIN, AND REPENTANCE, WERE DECLARED OPENLY IN THE EARLY HOURS OF AMERICAN HISTORY— WHEN REVIVALS AND AWAKENINGS SPREAD ACROSS OUR LANDSCAPE—"THE PULPITS WERE AFLAME WITH RIGHTEOUSNESS."

The gospel—the good news that Jesus came to save sinners—is an insult to the world. Jesus said that His message of redemption would not be popular, but that it would be an offense to the world. For this reason, some cautioned me that this chapter would hurt the marketability of my book; but responsibility, not marketability, is my goal. Most people respect the truth and are hungry for it. *We are to do what is right because it's right, not because it's popular.* Jesus spoke the truth because of His love for the lost; we should seek to do the same. "To convince the world of the truth of Christianity, it must first be convinced of sin. It is only sin that renders Christ intelligible" (Andrew Murray). "The proud, self-justifying, self-reliant, self-seeking self has to come simply as a lost, undone sinner, whose only hope is a justifying Savior" (Norman Grubb).

Foundational doctrines such as the cross, sin, and repentance, were declared openly in the early hours of American history—when revivals and awakenings spread across our landscape—"the pulpits were aflame with righteousness." Today, these foundational truths have been neglected, watered-down, or avoided altogether in the hope of "not offending," "securing an audience," or being "user-friendly." *Judgment is never mentioned; repentance is never sought; and sin is often excused.* This can leave people confused and deceived because they believe in a cross-less Christianity that bears no resemblance to Jesus' sobering call to repentance. Repentance opens the lines of communication between God and man. Biblically speaking, if we are to see God change America, leaders must repent, and we must repent collectively as a nation. "You can be certain that at the forefront of every significant recovery from backsliding... the doctrine of repentance has been among the precious truths that God has quickened and used" (Richard Roberts).

> THIS CAN LEAVE PEOPLE CONFUSED AND DECEIVED BECAUSE THEY BELIEVE IN A CROSS-LESS CHRISTIANITY THAT BEARS NO RESEMBLANCE TO JESUS' SOBERING CALL TO REPENTANCE.

As America falls deeper into self-reliance and further from reliance on God, our need for Christ has never been greater. It's been said that one of the greatest mission fields in the world today is the United States. This is largely due to the fact that awe and respect for the Lord have been forgotten in America; yet, "The fear of the LORD is the beginning of wisdom and knowledge"

(Psalm 111:10; Proverbs 1:7); Jesus also confirmed this in Matthew 10:28. However, we don't want to focus solely on God's judgment and what can keep us from heaven; we should also reflect on God's goodness, love, mercy, and grace. *For God so loved the world that He gave His only begotten Son, that whosoever believes in Him shall not perish but have everlasting life* (John 3:16). Take a minute and really ponder that verse. It's been quoted so often that we sometimes miss the powerful, life-changing message: God loved us so much that He allowed His Son to die on a cross for our sins. This alone should inspire us to follow Him. **It is a fact that two words from Jesus—"Follow Me"—have changed more lives than all the words of famous men combined.**

Who is Jesus to you? How you answer this question is the difference between right and wrong, light and darkness, heaven and hell. When asked this question, the apostle Peter gave the correct response: "You are the Christ, the Son of the living God" (Matthew 16:16). Jesus himself confirmed this by saying: "I am the way, the truth, and the life. No one comes to the Father except through Me" (John 14:6). Seriously consider who and what you choose to follow. If you take only one thing from this book, I hope it's this: Man's way leads to a hopeless end—God's way leads to an endless hope. God has shown us the way, not through religion, but through a relationship. **It's not about what**

> MAN'S WAY LEADS TO A HOPELESS END— GOD'S WAY LEADS TO AN ENDLESS HOPE. GOD HAS SHOWN US THE WAY, NOT THROUGH RELIGION, BUT THROUGH A RELATIONSHIP.

we do, but what He did on the cross. It's not about our righteousness but His!

If you feel that your relationship with Christ is not genuine, or if you've never truly repented and trusted in Him as your Lord and Savior, now is the time to take that step and fully commit your life. It's also important for many of us to recall 2 Chronicles 7:14, *If God's people will humble themselves and pray and seek His face and turn from their wicked ways, He will hear from heaven, forgive their sins, and heal their land.* **Without question, repentance, prayer, and humility before God is our only hope.**

If you're searching and not finding, hurting and not healing, and living but not loving, I encourage you to look to the One who has the answers and commit your life to Him. No matter what you have done or have experienced, you have the ability to start anew by turning to Christ. One famous quote captures it well: "A true measure of a person is not who they were, but who they will become." **It's all about Who you know—it's not too late—He is our only hope!**

Group
Study Questions

1. What does this quote say about the spiritual health of early America: *Not until I went to the churches of America and heard her pulpits aflame with righteousness did I understand the secret of her success?*

2. Comment on A.W. Tozer's quote: "Where does Christianity destroy itself in a given generation? It destroys itself by not living in the light, by professing a truth it does not obey."

3. Are we to do what is right because it's right, or because it's popular? Elaborate.

4. Why were the foundational doctrines of Christianity declared openly in the early hours of American history? Why are they so easily dispelled today?

5. What is the relationship between repentance and fulfilling the greatest commandment to love the Lord with all your heart, soul, strength, and mind?

6. What are some characteristics of a truly repentant person? What are some characteristics of a nation whose people have repented?

7. Have you truly repented and trusted in Christ as your Lord and Savior? It's not too late! (For more information, refer to Religion v. Relationship, at the end of the book.)

RESPONSE

1. _____
   _____
   _____

2. _____
   _____
   _____

3. _____
   _____
   _____

4. _____
   _____
   _____

5. _____
   _____
   _____

6. _____
   _____
   _____

7. _____
   _____
   _____

"Blessed is the nation whose God is the LORD"
(Psalm 33:12).

RECOMMENDED RESOURCES

Repentance: The First Word of the Gospel, by Richard Owen Roberts, unfolds the nature and necessity of true biblical repentance. Mr. Roberts also identifies the fruit that accompanies genuine repentance.

Can God Bless America?, by John MacArthur, lists several biblical conditions that must be met in order for God to truly bless America.

The Cross, by Martyn Lloyd-Jones, explains how Christ's crucifixion provided our redemption, and why this event is the cornerstone of the Christian faith.

The Root of the Righteous, by A.W. Tozer, taps into the bedrock of true spirituality. "If a sermon can be compared to light, then A.W. Tozer released a laser beam from the pulpit, a beam that penetrates your heart" (Warren Wiersbe).

Reflection & Journaling

Date _____

Additional Thoughts & Chapter Highlights

_____
_____
_____
_____
_____
_____
_____
_____
_____
_____
_____
_____

Prayers & Practical Application

_____
_____
_____
_____
_____
_____
_____
_____
_____
_____
_____
_____
_____

"I sat next to John Adams in Congress, and upon my whispering to him and asking him if he thought we should succeed in our struggle with Great Britain, he answered me, 'Yes—if we fear God and repent of our sins.' "[32]

—BENJAMIN RUSH (1745-1813)
Signer of the *Declaration of Independence*

Our American Birthright

By Roy Moore, former Chief Justice of the Supreme Court of Alabama—from his book, *So Help Me God*. Permission granted by *Foundation for Moral Law*.

One Nation under God was their cry and declaration,
Upon the law of Nature's God they built a mighty Nation.
For unlike mankind before them who had walked this
    earthen sod,
These men would never question the Sovereignty of God.

That all men were "created" was a truth "self-evident,"
To secure the rights God gave us was the role of
    government.
And if any form of government became destructive of
    this end,
It was their right, indeed their duty, a new one to begin.

So with a firm reliance on Divine Providence for
    protection,
They pledged their sacred honor and sought His wise
    direction.
They lifted up an appeal to God for all the world to see,
And vowed their independence forever to be free.

I'm glad they're not here with us to see the mess we're in,
How we've given up our righteousness for a life of
indulgent sin.
For when abortion isn't murder and sodomy is deemed a
right,
Then evil is now called good and darkness is now called
light.

**While truth and law were founded on the God of
all creation,
Man now, through law, denies the truth and
calls it "separation."**
No longer does man see a need for God when he's in full
control,
For the only truth self-evident is in the latest poll.

But with man as his own master we fail to count the cost,
Our precious freedoms vanish and our liberty is lost.
Children are told they can't pray in school and they teach
them evolution,
When will they see the fear of God is the only true
solution?

Our schools have become a battleground while all across
the land,
Christians shrug their shoulders afraid to take a stand.
And from the grave their voices cry, the victory has
already been won.
Just glorify the Father as did His only Son.

And when your work on earth is done, and you've
traveled where we've trod,
You'll leave the land we left to you, One Nation Under
God!

"My only hope of salvation is in the infinite transcendent love of God manifested to the world by the death of his Son upon the Cross."[33]

—BENJAMIN RUSH (1745-1813)

"I conjure you, by all that is dear, by all that is honorable, by all that is sacred, not only that ye pray but that ye act."[34]

—JOHN HANCOCK (1737-1793)
Signer of the *Declaration of Independence*

"It behooves us then to humble ourselves before the offended Power, to confess our national sins and to pray for clemency and forgiveness."

—ABRAHAM LINCOLN (1809-1865)
Proclamation of a National Fast, 1863

"It is true that religion has been closely identified with our history and government. As we said in Engle v. Vitale, 'The history of man is inseparable from the history of religion.' "

—UNITED STATES SUPREME COURT
Abington v. Schempp, 1963

"In this age there can be no substitute for Christianity. That was the religion of the founders of the republic, and they expected it to remain the religion of their descendants."[35]

—HOUSE & SENATE JUDICIARY COMMITTEE
Reports Taken Between 1853-1854

"Our citizens should early understand that the genuine source of correct republican principles is the Bible, particularly the New Testament, or the Christian religion."[36]

—NOAH WEBSTER (1758-1843)
Founding Father of American Education

"The propitious smiles of Heaven can never be expected on a nation that disregards the eternal rules of order and right which Heaven itself has ordained."[37]

—GEORGE WASHINGTON (1732-1799)
Inaugural Address, 1789

"Men, in a word, must necessarily be controlled either by a power within them or by a power without them; either by the Word of God or by the strong arm of man; either by the Bible or by the bayonet."[38]

—ROBERT WINTHROP (1809-1894)
Speaker of the U.S. House

"In those days politics were preached in the pulpits and men were led to action on the side of freedom by faithful pastors."

—BENSON J. LOSSING (1813-1891)
19TH Century Historian

"Whereas true religion and good morals are the only solid foundations of public liberty and happiness . . . it is hereby earnestly recommended to the several States to take the most effectual measures for the encouragement thereof."[39]

—CONTINENTAL CONGRESS, 1778

"Why may not the Bible, and especially the New Testament be read and taught as a divine revelation in the [school]? Where can the purest principles of morality be learned so clearly or so perfectly as from the New Testament?"[40]

—*VIDAL v. GIRARD'S* EXECUTORS
Philadelphia, 1844

"I do not believe that the Constitution was the offspring of inspiration, but I am as perfectly satisfied that the Union of the States, in its form and adoption, is as much the work of a Divine Providence as any of the miracles recorded in the Old and New Testament . . . ."[41]

—BENJAMIN RUSH (1745-1813)
Signer of the *Declaration of Independence*

"Our Constitution was made only for a moral and religious people. It is wholly inadequate to the government of any other."[42]

—JOHN ADAMS (1735-1826)
2ND President of the United States

"The origination and descent of all human power [is] from God first, to terrify evil doers; secondly, to cherish those who do well. Government seems to me to be a part of religion itself."[43]

—WILLIAM PENN (1644-1718)
Founder of Pennsylvania

"The foundations of our society and our government rest so much on the teachings of the Bible that it would be difficult to support them if faith in these teachings would cease to be practically universal in our country."[44]

—CALVIN COOLIDGE (1872-1933)
30TH President of the United States

"Our laws and our institutions must necessarily be based upon and embody the teachings of the Redeemer of mankind. It is impossible that it should be otherwise. In this sense and to this extent, our civilizations and our institutions are emphatically Christian."

—*RICHMOND v. MOORE*
Illinois Supreme Court, 1883

"All scholars shall live religious, godly, and blameless lives according to the rules of God's Word, diligently reading the Holy Scriptures . . . ."[45]

—REQUIREMENTS OF YALE COLLEGE, 1701

"No one should be afraid to take on any enterprise in the name of our Savior if it is right and if the purpose is purely for His holy service . . . ."[46]

—CHRISTOPHER COLUMBUS (1451-1506)
Credited with the Discovery of America

"Having undertaken [this endeavor] for the glory of God and advancement of the Christian faith . . . ."

—MAYFLOWER COMPACT
Considered America's First Constitution, 1620

"We shall be a city upon a hill, the eyes of all people are upon us; so that if we shall deal falsely with our God in this work we have undertaken, and so cause Him to withdraw His present help from us, we shall be made a story and a byword through the world."[47]

—JOHN WINTHROP (1588-1649)
One of the Recognized Leaders of the Puritans

SCRIPTURES IN REVIEW

Several key scriptures found throughout the book are listed on the following pages. These paraphrased Scriptures can be used for reference as you journal, and are reminders of the truth found in God's Word. Unfortunately, we often view the Bible only as a book of "dos and don'ts," rather than a book that contains absolute truth.

2 Chronicles 7:14
If My people will humble themselves and pray and seek My face and turn from their wicked ways, I will hear from heaven, forgive their sins, and heal their land.

Judges 2:10
And there arose another generation after them who did not know the LORD.

Isaiah 5:20
Woe be to those who call evil good, and good evil.

Psalm 11:3
If the foundations of righteousness and morality are destroyed, what can the righteous do?

Isaiah 7:9
If you do not stand strong in your faith and convictions, you will not be able stand at all.

Psalm 10:4

The arrogant man does not seek God—God is in none of his thoughts.

Psalm 12:8

The wicked freely parade and prance about while evil is praised throughout the land.

Ezekiel 22:30

God looked for a man from among the leaders who would build a wall and stand in the gap before Him on behalf of the land that He might not destroy it, but He found no one.

Jeremiah 1:5

Before I created you in the womb I knew you.

Psalm 139:13

God formed my inward parts; He knit me together in my mother's womb.

Psalm 82:3-4

Defend the weak and the fatherless, maintain the rights of the poor and oppressed, and deliver them from the hand of the wicked.

Deuteronomy 28:1

If you diligently obey the voice of the LORD and observe all that He has commanded you, He will set you high above all the nations of the earth.

Proverbs 11:3

Integrity and honesty will guide you continually.

2 Peter 1:5
A life of moral excellence and integrity leads to knowing God better.

2 Samuel 23:3
He who is a leader, and who rules over men, must be just.

Proverbs 14:34
Righteousness exalts and honors a nation, but sin is a reproach to any people.

Proverbs 1:7
The fear of the LORD is the beginning of wisdom and knowledge.

John 3:16
For God so loved the world that He gave His only Son, that whosoever believes in Him shall not perish but have everlasting life.

John 14:6
Jesus is the only way, the only truth, and the only life. No one comes to the Father except through Him.

"Many of the white people have been instruments in the hands of God for our good, even such as have held us in captivity, [and] are now pleading our cause with earnestness and zeal."

—RICHARD ALLEN (1760-1831)
Former Slave from Pennsylvania

The Founding Fathers and Slavery

THIS APPENDIX IS INTENDED TO point to those men who opposed the horrific practice of slavery. Although controversy surrounds some of them, their words reflect the heart of many of the Founders.

A special thanks to many of my African American friends who encouraged me to include this appendix, and to David Barton (WallBuilders) for allowing me to quote from his article: The Founding Fathers and Slavery. The following pages include a few important excerpts from his article:

Even though the issue of slavery is often raised as a discrediting charge against the Founding Fathers, the historical fact is that slavery was not the product of, nor was it an evil introduced by, the Founding Fathers; slavery had been introduced to America nearly two centuries before the Founders. As President of Congress Henry Laurens explained:

> I abhor slavery. I was born in a country where slavery had been established by British Kings and Parliaments as well as by the laws of the country ages before my existence . . . .[48]

The Revolution was the turning point in the national attitude [about slavery]—and it was the Founding Fathers who contributed greatly to that change. In fact, many of the Founders vigorously complained against the fact that Great Britain had forcefully imposed upon the Colonies the evil of slavery. For example, Thomas Jefferson heavily criticized that British policy:

> He [King George III] has waged cruel war against human nature itself, violating its most sacred rights of life and liberty in the persons of a distant people who never offended him, captivating and carrying them into slavery in another hemisphere or to incur miserable death in their transportation thither . . . . Determined to keep open a market where men should be bought and sold, he has prostituted his negative for suppressing every legislative attempt to prohibit or to restrain this execrable commerce [that is, he has opposed efforts to prohibit the slave trade].[49]

Benjamin Franklin, in a 1773 letter to Dean Woodward, confirmed that whenever the Americans had attempted to end slavery, the British government had indeed thwarted those attempts. Franklin explained that . . .

> . . . a disposition to abolish slavery prevails in North America, that many of Pennsylvanians have set their slaves at liberty, and that even the Virginia Assembly have petitioned the King for permission to make a law for preventing the importation of more into that colony. This request, however, will probably not be granted as their former laws of that kind have always been repealed.[50]

Further confirmation that even the Virginia Founders were not responsible for slavery, but actually tried to dismantle the institution, was provided by John Quincy Adams (known as the "hell-hound of abolition" for his extensive efforts against that evil). Adams explained:

> The inconsistency of the institution of domestic slavery with the principles of the Declaration of Independence was seen and lamented by all the southern patriots of the Revolution; by no one with deeper and more unalterable conviction than by the author of the Declaration himself [Jefferson]. No charge of insincerity or hypocrisy can be fairly laid to their charge. Never from their lips was heard one syllable of attempt to justify the institution of slavery. They universally considered it as a reproach fastened upon them by the unnatural step-mother country [Great Britain] and they saw that before the principles of the Declaration of Independence, slavery, in common with every other mode of oppression, was destined sooner or later to be banished from the earth. Such was the undoubting conviction of Jefferson to his dying day. In the Memoir of His Life, written at the age of seventy-seven, he gave to his countrymen the solemn and emphatic warning that the day was not distant when they must hear and adopt the general emancipation of their slaves.[51]

While Jefferson himself had introduced a bill designed to end slavery,[52] not all of the southern Founders were opposed to slavery. According to the testimony of Virginians James Madison, Thomas Jefferson, and John Rutledge, it was the Founders from North Carolina, South Carolina, and Georgia who most strongly favored slavery.[53]

Yet, despite the support for slavery in those States, the clear majority of the Founders opposed this evil. For instance, when some of the southern pro-slavery advocates invoked the Bible in support of slavery, Elias Boudinot, President of the Continental Congress, responded:

> [E]ven the sacred Scriptures had been quoted to justify this iniquitous traffic. It is true that the Egyptians held the Israelites in bondage for four hundred years, . . . but . . . gentlemen cannot forget the consequences that followed: they were delivered by a strong hand and stretched-out arm and it ought to be remembered that the Almighty Power that accomplished their deliverance is the same yesterday, today, and forever.[54]

Many of the Founding Fathers who had owned slaves as British citizens released them in the years following America's separation from Great Britain. Furthermore, many of the Founders had never owned any slaves. For example, John Adams proclaimed, "[M]y opinion against it [slavery] has always been known . . . [N]ever in my life did I own a slave."[55]

Notice a few additional examples of the strong anti-slavery sentiments held by great numbers of the Founders:

> [W]hy keep alive the question of slavery? It is admitted by all to be a great evil.[56]

> —CHARLES CARROLL,
> Signer of the Declaration

> That men should pray and fight for their own freedom and yet keep others in slavery is certainly acting a very

inconsistent, as well as unjust and perhaps impious, part.[57]

> —JOHN JAY,
> President of the Continental Congress,
> Original Chief Justice U.S. Supreme Court

I hope we shall at last, and if it so please God I hope it may be during my life time, see this cursed thing [slavery] taken out . . . . For my part, whether in a public station or a private capacity, I shall always be prompt to contribute my assistance towards effecting so desirable an event.[58]

> —WILLIAM LIVINGSTON,
> Signer of the Constitution;
> Governor of New Jersey

As much as I value a union of all the States, I would not admit the Southern States into the Union unless they agree to the discontinuance of this disgraceful trade [slavery].[59]

Honored will that State be in the annals of history which shall first abolish this violation of the rights of mankind.[60]

> —JOSEPH REED,
> Revolutionary Officer;
> Governor of Pennsylvania

Domestic slavery is repugnant to the principles of Christianity . . . . It is rebellion against the authority of a common Father. It is a practical denial of the extent and efficacy of the death of a common Savior . . . .[61]

> —BENJAMIN RUSH,
> Signer of the Declaration

> Justice and humanity require it [the end of slavery]–
> Christianity commands it. Let every benevolent . . .
> pray for the glorious period when the last slave who
> fights for freedom shall be restored to the possession
> of that inestimable right.[62]
>
> —NOAH WEBSTER

For many of the Founders, their feelings against slavery went beyond words. For example, in 1774, Benjamin Franklin and Benjamin Rush founded America's first anti-slavery society; John Jay was president of a similar society in New York.

Other prominent Founding Fathers who were members of societies for ending slavery included Richard Bassett, James Madison, James Monroe, Bushrod Washington, Charles Carroll, William Few, John Marshall, Richard Stockton, Zephaniah Swift, and many more. In fact, based in part on the efforts of these Founders, Pennsylvania and Massachusetts began abolishing slavery in 1780;[63] Connecticut and Rhode Island did so in 1784;[64] Vermont in 1786;[65] New Hampshire in 1792;[66] New York in 1799;[67] and New Jersey did so in 1804.[68] Additionally, the reason that Ohio, Indiana, Illinois, Michigan, Wisconsin, and Iowa all prohibited slavery was a Congressional act, authored by Constitution signer Rufus King[69] and signed into law by President George Washington,[70] which prohibited slavery in those territories.[71] It is not surprising that Washington would sign such a law, for it was he who had declared:

> I can only say that there is not a man living who wishes
> more sincerely than I do to see a plan adopted for the
> abolition of it [slavery].[72]

The truth is that it was the Founding Fathers who were responsible for planting and nurturing the first seeds for the recognition of black equality and for the eventual end of slavery. This was a fact made clear by Richard Allen.

Allen had been a slave in Pennsylvania but was freed after he converted his master to Christianity. Allen, a close friend of Benjamin Rush and several other Founding Fathers, went on to become the founder of the A.M.E. Church in America. In an early address "To the People of Color," he explained:

> Many of the white people have been instruments in the hands of God for our good, even such as have held us in captivity, [and] are now pleading our cause with earnestness and zeal.[73]

While much progress was made by the Founders to end the institution of slavery, unfortunately what they began was not fully achieved until generations later. Yet, despite the strenuous effort of many Founders to recognize in practice that "all men are created equal," charges persist to the opposite. In fact, revisionists even claim that the Constitution demonstrates that the Founders considered one who was black to be only three-fifths of a person. This charge is yet another falsehood. The three-fifths clause was not a measurement of human worth; rather, it was an anti-slavery provision to limit the political power of slavery's proponents. By including only three-fifths of the total number of slaves in the congressional calculations, Southern States were actually being denied additional pro-slavery representatives in Congress.

To review this article in its entirety, and others, including: *George Washington, Thomas Jefferson & Slavery in Virginia,* and *Thomas Jefferson and Sally Hemings: The Search for Truth,* visit the *Issues & Articles* link at www.wallbuilders.com in the *Library* section.

ABOUT THE AUTHOR

SHANE IDLEMAN'S PASSION FOR GOD'S WORD may well have been planted nearly 400 years ago when the Pilgrims first set foot on American soil. Interestingly, family tradition holds that Shane's maternal lineage can be traced to William White (1591-1621), the eleventh signer of the *Mayflower Compact*.

As the *Mayflower Compact* was signed in Cape Cod Harbor, it's not unreasonable to believe that the signers committed America to God's guidance, and asked that their children and grandchildren would carry biblical principles into each generation. Shane not only believes his passion may be in answer to that prayer spoken in the early hours of America's history, but he also believes that the spiritual baton is to pass from one generation to the next. He challenges the reader to be a pillar that supports the truth in their generation.

Today, as we continually drift away in a current of moral decay, many believe the battle is too advanced and that we cannot make a difference. Shane, however, believes we can, and offers this book as a contribution to that commitment. He currently resides in Southern California with his wife and children.

Other books by the author include:

What Works for Young Adults—Solid Choices in Unstable Times answers the top questions on the minds of young adults today such as: What is truth? How can I know God? Do all paths lead to heaven? What is God's will for my life? . . . and many more. Group study questions included. (190 pages)

What Works for Men—Regaining Lost Ground is a challenging, biblically based resource for men. (160 pages)

What Works for Singles—for Relationships, for Marriage, for Life is a motivational, biblically based resource for those divorced, those marrying for the first time, and those currently single. (200 pages)

What Works When "Diets" Don't will prepare you for the weight-loss process, motivate you to continue, and empower you to succeed while helping you reach your weight-loss goal in the shortest, safest amount of time. (232 pages)

Visit us at www.elpaseopublications.com

RELIGION v. RELATIONSHIP

A Personal Note From the Author

As a young, Southern California corporate executive for the fastest growing fitness company in the world in the mid-1990s, I had the opportunity to experience the devastating effects of life in the fast lane without rules or boundaries. As a result, I often went with the flow of society and focused on everything that the world had to offer.

Throughout my 20s, I continued to run from God; searching for identity and truth in everything but His Word. By age 28, I had climbed the corporate ladder. Money and success became my gods and ultimately controlled my life. **I was driven, but for the wrong reasons. I felt a sense of purpose, but it often left me feeling empty. I was passionate, but for the wrong things.** As a result of my misguided focus, my life took several unnecessary turns for the worse. By then, alcohol, anger, and arrogance had taken their toll—my life was crumbling around me. At that time, I believed I was strong because I could bench-press over 400 pounds, drink a 12-pack of beer, and win most of the fights I was in. What I failed to realize was that I was weak; I was dying spiritually. I didn't have control of my life—my life had control of me.

Sometime later, still unfulfilled, depressed, and desperate for direction, I began to thumb through the pages of my Bible that was shelved long ago. As I read, two Scriptures seemed to jump from the pages: *What does it profit you to gain the whole world but lose your soul?* (Luke 9:25), and, *When you hear God's voice do not harden your heart against Him* (Psalm 95:7-8). I suddenly realized just how far I had drifted from the truth. I was at a turning point. I could choose to humble myself, regain lost ground, and turn to God, or continue to reject Him. By God's grace, I put my complete trust in Him; joy, happiness, and peace filled my heart. Within the months that followed, my passion and purpose for life became clearer than ever.

> RELIGION FOCUSES ON WHAT "WE" DO; A RELATIONSHIP WITH CHRIST FOCUSES ON WHAT "HE" DID.

Looking back, I realize that I had *religion* but not a *relationship*. I lived, in what many would consider, a good Christian home. I attended a Christian school, went to a Christian church, and read the Bible from time to time, but I was confusing religion and rules with a true relationship with Christ. I thought I was a Christian because I was basically a good person. This is a major distinction between religion and a relationship. Religion focuses on what "we" do; a relationship with Christ focuses on what "He" did.

• Religion says, "I have to follow rules." A relationship says, "Because of the price He paid for me, I want to follow His plan."

- Religion says, "I have to go to church." A relationship says, "I want to learn more, worship Him, and benefit from fellowship."

- Religion lacks assurance; a relationship with Jesus offers unfailing guidance and assurance.

- Religion is man's attempt to reach God; a relationship with Christ is God reaching down to man.

> "THERE IS NO PEACE UNTIL WE SEE THE FINISHED WORK OF JESUS CHRIST—UNTIL WE CAN LOOK BACK AND SEE THE CROSS OF CHRIST BETWEEN OUR SINS"
>
> (D.L. MOODY).

Good is never good enough. We are declared right before God when we put our trust in Christ, not in our "good" works. This is often referred to as justification *by grace through faith alone*. In passages where Jesus referred to helping those in need, following Him unconditionally, and dying to self, *He was not saying that we are saved because we do these things, but rather, we do these things because we are saved.* "My good works grow out of God's working within me" (J.I. Packer).

Is your current belief system producing assurance, purpose, and peace, or is it bringing discouragement, disappointment, and despair? Jesus said that *wisdom is proved to be right by what results from it* (Matthew 11:19). Who, or what, is leading you—religious tradition, or a relationship with Jesus Christ? "There is no peace until we see the finished work of Jesus Christ—until we can look back and see the cross of Christ between our sins" (D.L. Moody).

Why do so many leave Sunday morning church services no different than when they arrived? Often, it's because they have religion and not a true relationship with Jesus. No wonder Jesus said that *many people draw near to Him with their words, but their hearts are far from Him* (Matthew 15:8). A.W. Tozer states it well: "Millions of professed believers talk as if [Christ] were real and act as if He were not. And always our actual position is to be discovered by the way we act, not by the way we talk."

In the New Testament, Jesus had harsh words for those who appeared to be religious but inwardly had not repented and changed. Our actions, not our words, reveal the authenticity of our relationship with Christ. I don't say this to promote a performance-based religion; I say it to demonstrate the importance of having a loyal, committed, genuine relationship with Jesus—this is how real change occurs. In Matthew 7:13, Jesus commanded us *to enter by the narrow gate, as opposed to walking through the wide gate that leads to destruction.* **Jesus was demonstrating the importance of having a personal relationship with Him, rather than following the crowd, religious tradition, or the latest fad.**

In my opinion, people often reject the Bible and a relationship with Jesus Christ not because they lack facts, but because they do not want to surrender their will and give up the so-called "good life"; they don't want there to be a God. **It's often an issue of the heart, not the intellect.**

We are sinners who need a Savior, but in our pride and arrogance we often reject God's gift. Jesus came to seek and to save that which was lost. Hebrews 9:22 says that *without the shedding of blood, there is no removal of sin.* His blood was shed for our sins; we should be forever thankful. **Jesus isn't an option; He's the way, the truth, and the life (John 14:6).**

As a word of encouragement to those who are struggling, consider this comparison I heard sometime ago. A pig and a lamb both find their way to the mud. The mud represents the sin we all fall into from time to time. The pig wallows in and enjoys the mud, and may even lead others in; the lamb hates its condition and cries out. That's the difference. Do you continually return and enjoy wallowing in sin, or do you regret and hate your condition when you slip into sin? The person who has made sin a lifestyle enjoys the sin; a follower of Christ regrets it, does what he or she can to avoid it, and cries out for forgiveness when stuck. *It's not about perfection but direction.*

> FORGET YOUR PAST MISTAKES, BUT REMEMBER THE LESSONS LEARNED BECAUSE OF THEM.

Although we've discussed personal choices and things we can do, we cannot forget the fact that we don't choose God as if He's sitting in heaven waiting to be chosen. He chooses us. He invites us. He calls us. In John 6:44 Jesus said, "No one can come to Me unless the Father who sent Me draws him." The relationship between God's sovereignty and man's responsibility is interwoven throughout the Scriptures. Our responsibility is to repent and believe, and to live a life that reflects that decision. Granted, life will seem unclear and confusing at times, but God promises that He will guide you. Don't let discouragement and failure stand in your way. I could write an entire book on my failures, but instead I strive to follow the apostle Paul's advice and I encourage you to do the same: *Forget about those things that are behind you. Instead reach forward to those things that are ahead of you* (Philippians 3:13). Forget your past mistakes, but remember the lessons learned because of them.

If you feel that your relationship with Christ is not genuine, or if you've never repented and trusted in Him as your Lord and Savior, now is the time to take that step and fully commit your entire life. Romans 10:9 states that "if you confess with your mouth the Lord Jesus and believe in your heart that God has raised Him from the dead, you will be saved." You don't want to live, or end, your life with a question mark here.

RECOMMENDED READING FOR SPIRITUAL GROWTH

Why Grace Changes Everything by Chuck Smith

Hard to Believe by John MacArthur

The Best of A.W. Tozer compiled by Warren W. Wiersbe

Disciplines of a Godly Man by R. Kent Hughes (for men)

How to Pray by R.A. Torrey

The Jesus Style by Gayle Erwin

The Case for Christ by Lee Strobel

The Kingdom of the Cults by Walter Martin

A Ready Defense by Josh McDowell

ENDNOTES

1. On March 30, 1863, Abraham Lincoln issued a historic *Proclamation Appointing a National Fast Day*. The quote, in its entirety, is as follows: "But we have forgotten God. We have forgotten the gracious Hand which preserved us in peace, and multiplied and enriched and strengthened us; and we have vainly imagined, in the deceitfulness of our hearts, that all these blessings were produced by some superior wisdom and virtue of our own."

2. This statement was made on December 23, 1866, when Henry Wilson spoke to the Y.M.C.A. at Natick, Massachusetts. The quote, in its entirety, is as follows: "Remember ever, and always, that your country was founded, not by the 'most superficial, the lightest, the most irreflective of all European races,' but by the stern old Puritans who made the deck of the Mayflower an altar of the living God, and whose first act on touching the soil of the new world was to offer on bended knees thanksgiving to Almighty God."

3. Daniel Webster, *The Works of Daniel Webster* (Boston: Little, Brown, and Company, 1853), Vol. I, p.403. The quote begins with, "Besides, there is no nation on earth . . . ."

4. Benjamin Franklin's remarks were recorded by James Madison, *The Papers of James Madison,* Henry D. Gilpin, editor (Washington: Langtree and O'Sullivan, 1840), Vol. II, pp.984-986, June 28, 1787.

5. "It's Almost Too Late," *New Man Magazine*—interview with Josh McDowell, May/June, 2003, p.56.

6. A statement made by Woodrow Wilson campaigning for the presidency in 1911. Reference: Lyndon B. Johnson, *Public Papers of Presidents of the United States Containing the Public Messages, Speeches, and Statements of the President* (Washington, D.C.: Government Printing Office, 1965), Book II: July 1 to December 31, 1964, p.884.

7. After reviewing a surplus of information, the U.S. Supreme Court, in the *Church of the Holy Trinity v. United States,* came to this conclusion in 1892. The quote actually begins with: "But, beyond all these matters, no purpose of action against religion can be imputed to any legislation, state or national, because this is a religious people. This is historically true. From the discovery of this continent to the present hour, there is a single voice making this affirmation."

After referencing many historical proofs related to America's heritage, the Court continues: "These and many other matters which might be noticed, add a volume of unofficial declarations to the mass of organic utterances that this is a Christian nation."

8. John Quincy Adam's quote can be found in *The Jubilee of the Constitution* (New York: Published by Samuel Colman, 1839), pp. 13-14. The reference for the Bible's influence on the Founders can be found in Donald Lutz's work, *The Origins of American Constitutionalism,* (Baton Rouge, LA: Louisiana State University Press, 1988), p. 141. Additionally, see David Barton's book, *The Role of Pastors & Christians in civil government,* (WallBuilders, Inc. © 2003), p.17.

9. *Stone v. Graham,* 449 U.S. 39 (1980). Additionally: *Ring v. Grand Forks Public School District,* 483 F. Supp. 272 (D.C. ND 1980).

10. A quote from John Jay's last will and testament.

11. In 1995, Samuel B. Kent, U.S. District judge for the Southern District of Texas, made this decree.

12. Rosalie Slater, from an essay in the preface to a facsimile edition of Noah Webster's 1828 edition of *An American Dictionary of the English Language* (San Francisco, 1980), p.12.

13. *Constitutions* (1785), pp. 99-100, Delaware, 1776, Article 22. Additionally, see Morris, B.F., *Christian Life and Character of the Civil Institutions of the United States,* (Philadelphia, 1864), Chapter 11.

14. *Works of Fisher Ames,* Compiled by a Number of His Friends (Boston: T.B. Wait & Co, 1809), pp. 134-135, "School Books," First Published in the Palladium, January, 1801.

15. Benjamin Rush, *Essays, Literary, Moral and Philosophical* (Philadelphia: Thomas & Samuel F. Bradford, 1798), p.8, "Of the Mode of Education Proper in a Republic."

16. *Roberts v. Madigan,* 702 F. Supp. 1505 (D.C. Colo. 1989), 921 F. 2d 1047 (10 Cir. 1990), cert. denied, 112 S. Ct. 3025; 120 L. Ed. 2d 896.

17. John Adams, *Works* (1856), Vol. X, p.45, to Thomas Jefferson on June 28th, 1813.

18. Many acknowledge the fact that this quote is consistent with Henry's life and character even though it cannot be confirmed. It's possible that this unconfirmed quote came from Henry's uncle: Reverend Patrick Henry.

19. David Barton, www. wevotevalues.com/church clips info.html (October 22nd, 2004). Additionally, see *Vidal v. Girard's Executors,* 43 U.S. 126, 132 (1844).

20. Jared Sparks, in searching for information on Washington's religious habits, dispatched a letter to Nelly asking her about George Washington's faith. She replied to Sparks on February 26, 1833.

21. Jefferson, *Writings*, Vol. XVI, pp.281-282, to the Danbury Baptist Association dated January 1, 1802.

22. D. James Kennedy, Special Report—Truth & Tyranny, © 2003, p.1.

23. *People v. Ruggles*, 8 Johns 545 (Sup. Ct. NY. 1811).

24. The actual sign can be seen on the DVD, *The League of Grateful Sons*, by Vision Forum Ministries © 2005.

25. Inaugural Address, January 20, 1953; 34th president of the U.S. 1953-1961 (1890 - 1969).

26. D. James Kennedy, *The First Amendment on Trial,* June 2004, Coral Ridge Ministries Media newsletter, Inc., p.1, quoting Zell Miller in a Senate floor speech he presented on Feb. 12, 2004.

27. Jefferson, Thomas; 1781, *Notes on the State of Virginia,* Query xv111, 1781, 1782, p. 237.

28. Used by permission of The CS Lewis Company Ltd; © CS Lewis Pte Ltd.

29. Alexander Hamilton, *The Papers of Alexander Hamilton,* Harold C. Syrett, editor (New York: Columbia University Press, 1961), Vol. I, p.87, February 23, 1775, quoting William Blackstone, *Commentaries on the Laws of England,* Vol. I, p.41.

30. Moore, James P. Jr., *One Nation Under God—The History of Prayer in America,* (Doubleday, © 2005).

31. Richard Owen Roberts, *Repentance—the first word of the gospel,* (Published by Crossway Books © 2002), p.16.

32. Benjamin Rush, *Letters of Benjamin Rush,* L.H. Butterfield, editor (NJ: American Philosophical Society, 1951), Vol. I, pp.532-536, to John Adams on February 24, 1790.

33. Benjamin Rush, *The Autobiography of Benjamin Rush,* George W. Corner, editor (Princeton: Princeton University Press for the American Philosophical Society, 1948), p.166.

34. John R. Musick, *Great Americans of History—John Hancock* (Chicago: Union

School Furnishing Company 1898), pp.116-117.

35. *Reports of Committees of the House of Representatives Made During the First Session of the Thirty-Third Congress* (Washington: A.O.P. Nicholson, 1854), pp. 1, 6, 8-9. The quote, in its entirety, is as follows: ". . . In this age there can be no substitute for Christianity; that, in its general principles, is the great conservative element on which we must rely for the purity and permanence of free institutions. That was the religion of the founders of the republic, and they expected it to remain the religion of their descendants."

36. Noah Webster, *History of the United States* (New Haven: Durrie & Peck, 1832), p.6.

37. George Washington in his first inaugural address, April 30, 1789. The quote, in its entirety, is as follows: "We ought to be no less persuaded that the propitious smiles of Heaven can never be expected on a nation that disregards the eternal rules of order and right which Heaven itself has ordained . . . ."

38. Robert Winthrop, *Addresses and Speeches on Various Occasions* (Boston: Little, Brown and Co., 1852), p. 172, from an address delivered at the annual meeting of the Massachusetts Bible Society in Boston, May 28, 1849.

39. *Journals of the American Congress: From 1774 to 1788* (Washington: Way and Gideon, 1823), Vol. III, p.85, October 12, 1788.

40. *Vidal v Girard's Executors,* 43 U.S. 126, 200 (1844). The quote, with ellipses, is as follows: "Why may not the Bible, and especially the New Testament . . . be read and taught as a divine revelation in the [school]? . . . Where can the purest principles of morality be learned so clearly or so perfectly as from the New Testament?"

41. Benjamin Rush, *Letters of Benjamin Rush,* L.H. Butterfield, editor (Princeton, New Jersey: American Philosophical Society, 1951), Vol. I, p.475, to Elias Boudinot on July 9, 1788.

42. John Adams, *The Works of John Adams,* Charles Frances Adams, editor (Boston: Little, Brown and Company, 1854), Vol. IX, p. 229, to the Officers of the First Brigade of the Third Division of the Militia of Massachusetts on October 11, 1798.

43. William Penn; April 25, 1682, in the preface of his *Frame of Government of Pennsylvania.* The quote, with ellipses, is as follows: "The origination and descent of all human power [is] from God . . . first, to terrify evil doers; secondly, to cherish those who do well . . . . Government seems to me to be a part of religion itself."

44. (John) Calvin Coolidge; 1923, statement. Charles Fadiman, ed., *The American Treasury* (NY: Harper & Brothers, Publishers, 1955), p.127.

45. Yale College; 1701, Richard Hofstader and Wilson Smith, eds., *American Higher Education: A Documentary History* (Chicago, IL: University of Chicago Press, 1961), 1:49.

46. Christopher Columbus, *Christopher Columbus's Book of Prophecies,* Kay Brigham, translator (Barcelona, Spain: CLIE, 1990; Ft. Lauderdale: TSELF, 1991), pp. 178-179, 182-183.

47. John Winthrop, *The Winthrop Papers,* Stewart Mitchell, editor (Massachusetts Historical Society, 1931), Vol II, pp.292-295, "A Model of Christian Charity," 1630. The sentence actually starts with "For we must consider that we shall be a city upon a hill, the eyes of all people are upon us . . . ."

48. Frank Moore, *Materials for History Printed From Original Manuscripts, the Correspondence of Henry Laurens of South Carolina* (New York: Zenger Club, 1861), p. 20, to John Laurens on August 14, 1776.

49. Thomas Jefferson, *The Writings of Thomas Jefferson,* Albert Ellery Bergh, editor (Washington, D.C.: Thomas Jefferson Memorial Assoc., 1903), Vol. I, p. 34.

50. Benjamin Franklin, *The Works of Benjamin Franklin,* Jared Sparks, editor (Boston: Tappan, Whittemore, and Mason, 1839), Vol. VIII, p. 42, to the Rev. Dean Woodward on April 10, 1773.

51. John Quincy Adams, *An Oration Delivered Before The Inhabitants Of The Town Of Newburyport at Their Request on the Sixty-First Anniversary of the Declaration of Independence, July 4, 1837* (Newburyport: Charles Whipple, 1837), p. 50.

52. Jefferson, *Writings,* Vol. I, p. 4.

53. Jefferson, *Writings,* Vol. I, p. 28, from his autobiography; see also James Madison, *The Papers of James Madison* (Washington: Langtree and O'Sullivan, 1840), Vol. III, p. 1395, August 22, 1787; see also James Madison, *The Writings of James Madison*, Gaillard Hunt, editor, (New York: G.P. Putnam's Sons, 1910), Vol. IX, p. 2, to Robert Walsh on November 27, 1819.

54. *The Debates and Proceedings in the Congress of the United States* (Washington, D.C.: Gales and Seaton, 1834), First Congress, Second Session, p. 1518, March 22, 1790; see also George Adams Boyd, *Elias Boudinot, Patriot and Statesman* (Princeton, New Jersey: Princeton University Press, 1952), p. 182.

55. John Adams, *The Works of John Adams, Second President*

of the United States, Charles Francis Adams, editor (Boston: Little, Brown, and Company, 1854), Vol. IX, pp. 92-93, to George Churchman and Jacob Lindley on January 24, 1801.

56. Kate Mason Rowland, *Life and Correspondence of Charles Carroll of Carrollton* (New York & London: G.P. Putnam's Sons, 1898), Vol. II, p. 321, to Robert Goodloe Harper, April 23, 1820.

57. John Jay, *The Life and Times of John Jay,* William Jay, editor (New York: J. & S. Harper, 1833), Vol. II, p. 174, to the Rev. Dr. Richard Price on September 27, 1785.

58. William Livingston, *The Papers of William Livingston,* Carl E. Prince, editor (New Brunswick: Rutgers University Press, 1988), Vol. V, p. 358, to James Pemberton on October 20, 1788.

59. *Elliot's Debates* (Washington: Printed for the Editor, 1836), Vol. III, pp. 452-454, George Mason, June 15, 1788.

60. William Armor, *Lives of the Governors of Pennsylvania* (Norwich, Conn.: T.H. Davis & Co., 1874), p. 223.

61. Benjamin Rush, *Minutes of the Proceedings of a Convention of Delegates from the Abolition Societies Established in Different Parts of the United States Assembled at Philadelphia* (Philadelphia: Zachariah Poulson, 1794), p. 24.

62. Noah Webster, *Effect of Slavery on Morals and Industry* (Hartford: Hudson and Goodwin, 1793), p. 48.

63. *A Constitution or Frame of Government Agreed Upon by the Delegates of the People of the State of Massachusetts-Bay* (Boston: Benjamin Edes and Sons, 1780), p. 7, Article I, "Declaration of Rights" and An Abridgement of the Laws of Pennsylvania, Collinson Read, editor, (Philadelphia: Printed for the Author, 1801), pp. 264-266, Act of March 1, 1780.

64. *The Public Statue Laws of the State of Connecticut* (Hartford: Hudson and Goodwin, 1808), Book I, pp. 623-625, Act passed in October 1777 and Rhode Island Session Laws (Providence: Wheeler, 1784), pp. 7-8, Act of February 27, 1784.

65. *The Constitutions of the Sixteen States* (Boston: Manning and Loring, 1797), p. 249, Vermont, 1786, Article I, "Declaration of Rights."

66. *Constitutions* (1797), p. 50, New Hampshire, 1792, Article I, "Bill of Rights."

67. *Laws of the State of New York, Passed at the Twenty-Second Session, Second Meeting of the Legislature* (Albany: Loring Andrew, 1798), pp. 721-723, Act passed on March 29, 1799.

68. *Laws of the State of New Jersey, Compiled and Published Under the Authority of the*

Legislature, Joseph Bloomfield, editor (Trenton: James J. Wilson, 1811), pp. 103-105, Act passed February 15, 1804.

69. Rufus King, *The Life and Correspondence of Rufus King,* Charles King, editor (New York: G.P. Putnam's Sons, 1894), Vol. I, pp. 288-289.

70. *Acts Passed at a Congress of the United States of America* (Hartford: Hudson and Goodwin, 1791), p. 104, August 7, 1789.

71. *The Constitutions of the United States* (Trenton: Moore and Lake, 1813), p. 366, "An Ordinance for the Government of the Territory of the United States Northwest of the River Ohio," Article VI.

72. George Washington, *The Writings of George Washington,* John C. Fitzpatrick, editor (Washington, D.C.: Government Printing Office, 1932), Vol. XXVIII, pp. 407-408, to Robert Morris on April 12, 1786.

73. Richard Allen, *The Life Experience and Gospel Labors of the Right Rev. Richard Allen* (Nashville: Abingdon Press, 1983), p. 73, from his "Address to the People of Color in the United States."